Go it
ALONE

RICHARD GREENSTED

Go it ALONE

How to break

free of wage slavery

and become a

micro-entrepreneur

PAN BOOKS

First published 1995 by Pan Books
an imprint of Macmillan General Books
Cavaye Place London SW10 9PG
and Basingstoke

Associated companies throughout the world

ISBN 0 333 62196 4

1 3 5 7 9 8 6 4 2

A CIP catalogue record for this book is available from
the British Library

Typeset by CentraCet Limited, Cambridge
Printed and bound by Cox & Wyman Ltd, Reading, Berkshire

To my father

CONTENTS

INTRODUCTION

This is not a 'how to' book. Within these pages you will find no guidance on filling in your VAT return or producing an invoice. This is a 'whether to' book. Very few of us can claim never to have harboured a dream to work for ourselves, to break free and do our own thing. But fewer of us have actually taken the plunge, often into completely uncharted waters and oblivious to the perils that lie ahead. The objective of this book is to act as a reference guide to the cultural and psychological changes that confront those who are bold enough to believe that they can make it on their own. Not everyone is cut out for the life of a micro-entrepreneur: reading this book should help you to decide whether you are one of them.

The sole trader is assuming an enormous amount of influence in the global economy. As businesses strive to become leaner and fitter, they are reviewing each of the tasks they undertake, and are examining whether it would be more cost-effective to delegate many of these functions to external providers. The sole trader is well-placed to take advantage of these opportunities: with low overheads, and built-in flexibility, there are some compelling reasons to use a small operator.

To take advantage of these opportunities, and to build a business that is robust and well-positioned, requires a unique combination of skill and determination: sole traders must assume the role of chief executive, finance director, sales and marketing manager, client relations officer, and general factotum – a jack-of-all-trades and master of all! Sole traders report to the highest authority of all (at least in the world of business): the paying customer. For those of us inured to the ways of big business, where customers rarely enjoy such an exalted status, this cultural adjustment can be painful and difficult to manage. Freedom from the restraints of employee status is replaced by a new type of constraint, that of satisfying customer needs.

Before making the huge leap towards independence, it makes sense to have a clear idea of the risks and rewards involved. Government agencies and self-help manuals can give lots of useful advice on how to set up a business, how to prepare a budget and a forecast, and how to write your business plans. But those are not the only issues that you will face: equally important are the considerations of your own suitability for life in this exciting environment, where self-reliance is paramount and you have nobody to blame but yourself if things don't go according to plan. This book aims to redress that balance, raising some questions and providing some practical advice about how your life will change.

The best people to go to for advice are the people who've done it themselves, those who've gone through the agonies and ecstasies and have lived to tell the tale. That's why there are 10 case studies included in the book. Each one of them, I assure you, is absolutely genuine, and each of the interviewees was brutally frank about their experience and how they would have done things differently if they'd known then what they know now. There are some common themes running through the case studies: finance (or the lack of it), the need to plan ahead, the exhilaration of being in command of events, the despair of not getting paid when expected, and the feeling that, once you've embarked upon this wonderful adventure of self-employment, it soon becomes addictive. The combined knowledge and skill of these adventurers is well worth studying in great detail.

Perhaps you are standing in a bookshop as you read this, on your lunch break or at the end of the working day. You're at the early stages of considering a move away from employment by others: maybe you're frustrated by your current job, or you fear that the corporate axe will very shortly descend on your head. Whatever your motivation for thinking about life as a sole trader, you're unlikely to have any real idea of what's involved. You may have some friends who've done it, but they wouldn't be too keen on sharing their innermost hopes and fears with you. And an awful lot of what happens to the sole trader in the early days is quickly forgotten, especially when business starts to pick up and the money rolls in.

So, as you daydream in the bookshop, or at your desk, there should be a large flashing red light above your head. This is not a move for the faint-hearted: to succeed on your own will require reserves of determination and resolve that you never knew you had. You will suffer from set-backs, you will agonize over money, you will lose business you should have won, you will have to work twice as hard as ever before, and you will frequently reach the conclusion that it was all a dreadful mistake and you wish someone else was paying you a regular income. But . . . the rewards easily outweigh these horrors: you work to suit yourself, you plan to achieve objectives that you set, rather than targets set for you, you can change direction at the drop of a hat, you can choose your customers according to your own criteria, your potential to earn money is limited only by your own imagination and sweat and, if you get it right, there is a type of job satisfaction that you never dreamed was possible.

Even the most well-intentioned advice will have to be tailored to suit the individual, and I cannot claim that mine is any different. Every person I interviewed for the book has developed some unique experience that applies only to them, and you will only find out what works for you if you take the big step and start up on your own. But it is my hope that what is written here will ring some bells with every reader, and that, in the years to come when you're sitting on some palm-fringed beach with a cooling drink in your hand, you'll feel that some of the advice I've given was practical and useful.

Building your own business can be the greatest thrill there is, but it pays to go into it with a clear-eyed view of the pitfalls and problems that you'll undoubtedly encounter. Forewarned is forearmed – and I hope that this book will act as a little extra armour in the battles you'll face if you go it alone.

Chapter One

CULTURE SHOCK

For many of us, the two certainties of life – death and taxes – have been joined by a third: redundancy. In today's economic environment, only the most stubbornly Jurassic trade union bosses still believe in full employment and jobs for life; the rest of us are already facing up to the reality that our working lives are almost sure to be punctuated by periods of enforced idleness. Those still lucky enough to be in employment wonder when the axe will fall on their position, replaced by smarter technology and systems that don't ask for pensions and company cars.

Employers, in the curiously British style of management, are much nicer to you when they know you're leaving: they offer attractive incentives to go, and dull the pain with analgesic offerings of extended private health-care plans and the like. But, however laudable their motives might be, these soft-landing tactics are the worst thing to have when you lose your job. Redundancy is, and should be, a rude shock to the system and, if you are really convinced that you can work for yourself, it's the best thing that can happen to you. All the attendant financial incentives are merely a diversion, artlessly designed to blur your vision and reduce the impact of change in your life.

The Cruellest Cut

Let's consider the typical circumstances of a middle manager who faces 'corporate down-sizing' or similar euphemisms for losing one's job: the employer decides that the manager is dispensable. This in itself is a surprising revelation to most of us, who resolutely believe that our place in the organization is a vital cog in the wheels of industry, however small and poorly oiled. The manager is advised, more often by letter than face-to-face, and the package negotiations begin. The employer may offer some tax-free lump sum based on years of service, and may give an extended period before the car goes back, the cheap loans have to be repaid, the health insurance ceases, and other benefits are withdrawn. To the employer, this appears eminently fair and reasonable; to the employee, it's usually too little, and grossly unjust. But, right or wrong, the severance terms are agreed, and the manager, and the job, disappear.

What exactly is wrong with this settlement? The first problem is that it perpetuates the safety net that hangs beneath every employee, however precariously: the manager still thinks of the ex-employer as providing some comfort and support by way of benefits-in-kind. For those who are determined to start out on their own, this is a dangerous myth, which merely delays the day of reckoning when survival will be entirely dependent upon one's own abilities, cut free from the corporate matriarch. The sooner you realize that life is in earnest, the better: working for yourself quickly establishes the real priorities, like food, shelter and heat.

The second, and equally unfair, flaw in this arrangement is that the cash amount is nearly always denominated as a multiple of 'monthly salary'. For the newly redundant person, this has an iniquitous effect: it makes you think in terms of fixed time periods, which will quickly become irrelevant when you go into business for yourself. Work doesn't come to the self-employed in neatly packaged weekly or monthly cycles, and neither does cash. Every self-help book I've ever read implores the sole trader to plan ahead, to make cashflow forecasts, and run monthly budgets. Whilst this sounds sensible and prudent, for the new entrepreneur it is plainly absurd, attempting to predict the unpredictable and read the minds of customers you may never have met, let alone sold anything to. Of course you should have an overall view of how, when and where you will earn your living – but more on that later. What matters here is that the acceptance of three or six months' salary immediately triggers the thought: 'Thank God! At least I can keep going that long' – when in actual fact your whole view of how to survive, and what you need at the bare minimum, will have to change dramatically.

Starting from Zero

Those of us who have become accustomed to receiving regular payments from employers, electronically delivered into our bank accounts, get lazy about budgetary control. If you know you're going to be paid £2,000 every month, then that's what you'll spend – or more, if your bank manager lets you. This view of expenditure can be described as the 'top-down' approach: you start with a number, determined by the employer, and then find ways to disburse that amount for every period it continues to be paid. The sole trader adopts exactly the opposite approach – the 'bottom-up' theory – where there is no fixed payment, and expenditure plans start from point zero. The self-employed person looks not at income, but outgoings, first, and asks the question: 'What is the absolute minimum I can get by on?' There is nothing that focuses the mind so wonderfully as an empty bank account.

So the severance pay-off is really a distraction, delaying the realization that no more cash will be magically credited to your account. Worse than that, it engenders a feeling of wealth: for many of us, this tax-free payment is one of the largest single credits we will ever see on our bank statement, and a healthy credit balance is an unhealthy temptation – to buy equipment we don't need, to rent offices we can't afford, to hire staff we don't require. The best thing to do with any significant severance payment is – nothing. Put it in a high-interest account, give it to your mum to look after, put it into gilts – but keep it separate from your day-to-day expenditure. If you want to succeed on your own, do it from day one. This advice is easy to give, much

more difficult to take – but who said working for yourself was
going to be easy?

The Land of the Brave

At the point when your desk is cleared, and the leaving drinks are
over, you may already have some vague notion of what to do
next. Perhaps you've tried – and failed – to get another job. If
you're really lucky, the ex-employer may be paying for 'career
counselling', which may clarify the likelihood of ever being
employed again. Don't underestimate the value of this counselling, especially when someone else is paying for it: the better
counsellors can actually give you a lot of help in assessing your
strengths and weaknesses. Maybe you've toyed with the idea of
doing your own thing, being your own boss, and ending up as a
successful and fulfilled entrepreneur, complete with chauffeured
limousine, mobile phone and several personal assistants. But few
people leave jobs, either voluntarily or otherwise, with a clear
vision of precisely how they will make their living as a sole trader.
A tiny minority have a brilliant idea, spot a gap in the market, fill
it successfully, and end up as multi-millionaires, and those that
do will not be reading this book! For most of us, the notion of
self-employment is both appealing and frightening, and we
stumble into it in the same way as a woman experiences her first
childbirth: if anyone had told her exactly how ghastly it was
going to be, she'd never have agreed to go through with it!

So the first thing to accept, as you sit with your partner and
listen to their commiserations, is that the prospect of self-
employment is not for the faint-hearted. It is not about designing
a product or service, and finding customers, and collecting
money, and managing growth – although all these things are
vitally important, of course – but it is about a complete and utter
reorganization and reappraisal of your values, your priorities,
your standards, your whole cultural approach to life and the
living of it. Working for yourself requires all this and more: the

sole trader is not a normal human being, tied umbilically to support systems provided by others. This independence is a double-edged sword: on the one side, it allows for total freedom of action in choosing what to do, when to do it, and with whom, but, on the other side, it creates enormous pressures (on family and friends as well as on the individual), continuing uncertainties, and the blackest of depressions and despair when things don't go well. Not everyone has the metabolism for it and, as yet, there is no medical test to determine suitability.

Some readers may already have closed this book, deterred by the darker side to life as a micro-entrepreneur. That is no bad thing: it is much better to know early that you cannot survive without the corporate support systems and someone else running the more mundane aspects of your life. You will have to start worrying about the cost of business phone calls, pension contributions, Customs and Excise, annual accounts, and all the other boring but necessary administrative details of being your own boss, if you really want to succeed for yourself. Becoming self-employed is as traumatic as leaving home for the first time, and finding that mum and dad aren't there any more to cook your breakfast, do your laundry and lend you money that you forget to repay. But the rewards are only limited by your own imagination and courage: liberation from the shackles of wage slavery is a powerful stimulant, and is frighteningly addictive.

Sadly, the first reaction of many friends and relatives to the merest suggestion that you might go it alone is normally a sharp intake of breath and the comment: 'That's very brave.' For 'brave', read 'stupid' – most people, especially amongst the older generations, have been brought up to perceive the self-employed as slightly unsavoury characters, like the cowboy plumber who never mends the washing machine properly, or as people who really can't do anything else. For a society dominated by the employer/employee relationship, and steeped in a tradition of workers and managers, the idea of self-employment is still regarded as risky, second-best, and unconventional. But society is changing, as technology supplants many of our manual and mental skills, and the sole trader is becoming an increasingly important contributor to the economic well-being of the country. None of this, of course, will help to convince your parents that you're making a smart move, but it is important to value your own place in society, and your contribution to it. If you can persuade yourself that being your own boss is not simply the only option available to you, but rather an active decision to control your own destiny and improve your lifestyle, you will have made a major step forward in shaping the attitude you will need to succeed on your own.

Talent Spotting

Even if you are convinced that self-employment is for you, there are still enormous hurdles to overcome. Putting aside money for one moment, there is the small question of what you will actually do to make it. For many salaried staff, the marzipan layer of British industry, the functions that they have always performed for employers seem of little or no value once in the outside world. Having a professional banking qualification, for instance, hardly equips you to establish your own bank. So many salaried jobs are entirely dependent on the company infrastructure that, stripped away from this, they seem worthless. But whatever you have done in a big company, there will be something that you can take away and use profitably when it comes to working for yourself. One of the biggest merits of working for someone else is that it imposes disciplines – deadlines must be met, reports must be written, goods delivered, bills paid – and these disciplines will be of immense value when it comes to doing everything for yourself. In a sense, this is what you learnt at school, when homework had to be done and tables memorized for tests and exams: the actual content of what you did was not necessarily as important as the routine it taught you to establish to achieve these things. To a greater or lesser extent, we all have to work to deadlines, even if it is only as mundane as catching a train every day. And time management, as we will see later, is of fundamental importance to the sole trader.

The danger, as mentioned earlier, is that you perceive self-employment as the main chance in the acquisition of real wealth. We've all seen Richard Branson in the news media, a paradigm for the budding entrepreneur with his apparently effortless creation of a thriving empire. But, unfortunately, life for most self-employed people is not like that, and it's well worth pointing out that the vast majority of sole traders live a hand-to-mouth existence, substantially satisfied by their working arrangements but far away from the world of Bermudan holidays and a new Mercedes in the drive. The expectations of the prospective entrepreneur must be realistic, and cannot be based on money alone. Self-employment may never bring substantial cash rewards, but it can deliver job satisfaction, a healthier state of mind, and a sense of self-esteem – not a bad set of criteria on which to build your life.

Advice on Advice

Undeterred, and ready for action, you're positive that you can effect the cultural adjustment, that your peers and allies have at least given you lukewarm support, and that the time is definitely right to be your own boss. Surprisingly, you will discover that there is an endless stream of advice from everyone – including the government. People you hardly know will freely give you their tips for success, and you will be inundated with counsel from the most unlikely sources. The best advice I can give is – listen to all the advice. Some will be rubbish, some will be usable, some will be brilliant: you'll have to rely on your own instincts about which is which, but you must never turn down free advice. When I was starting out on my own, I was bought lunch by a well-paid and extremely successful consultant. He asked me what I was going to do, and how I was going to do it. I tried hard to impress him with the clarity of my business plan and the focus of my target client base. He listened politely and, over coffee, gave me the best advice I have ever taken, free or paid-for: 'Be absolutely clear about what you want to do. But never rule out anything just because it doesn't fit in with your plan. Judge each opportunity on its merits.' He was right: I had ditched my original intentions within a year, because something better came along and I took it.

Even the government gives good advice. At another meeting in my early days as a sole trader, I went to see a small business adviser at the Department of Employment – at no charge. This man ran several small companies, and was clearly good at what he did. He listened to my plans, and told me to forget about all the paraphernalia of business – accountants, solicitors, offices, computers, staff – until I had a customer, a real, live, paying customer. Everything else would fall into place once I had proved to myself that I was selling something that people would buy. I followed his advice, and I'm still in business (and I still don't have a solicitor or an office!). One of the luxuries of self-employment is that you can listen to advice as much as you like, but the final decision rests with you. Don't be afraid to ask – people are naturally flattered when you seek their opinion, and will normally do their level best to give you a sensible response. It's up to you as to what you do with what they say, and that discretion is supremely satisfying. It is difficult to take advice. One of the reasons for this is that we get used to so much poor guidance from our managers, when we are employees, that we find it inconceivable that anyone (other than ourselves, of course!) actually knows what they're talking about. But there are people who do – and your job is to find them.

Mixed Emotions

Students of the human mind would have a field day with someone who was thinking of starting their own business, especially if that person had been made redundant. When your company 'lets you go' – an interesting euphemism, as if you'd asked and they'd kindly agreed – you are going to discover the whole gamut of emotions, from A to Z. Naturally you'll be furious: how could anybody think that you're expendable and dispensable? This fury often manifests itself with threats of legal action and other terrifying retributions. But the anger soon abates, to be replaced by depression: how will I live, what will I do, how will I ever get another job? When not depressed, there is likely to be an element of panic as you thrash around trying to imagine what life will be like without the corporate support systems. Then, as often as not, there is a period of elation as you realize that you are free to do as you wish. Suddenly nobody is telling you what to do; no one is handing you unpleasant work assignments and barking in your ear to get them completed. You no longer need to fight your way into work, or wear the stupid uniform of business.

Career counsellors will tell you that all this emotional journey is absolutely necessary if you are ever to get yourself sorted out, and I have to agree with them. If you have been made redundant it is very important that you clear out your emotional sinuses: it is only once you have done this that you will reach the stage where you're ready to face up to the future. You musn't be carrying any emotional baggage with you when you begin your new life as your own boss. You don't want to harbour grudges against your ex-employer, so get rid of the anger and move on. You certainly don't want to be depressed when you open up for business, and the panic should have been replaced by a clear-eyed focus on what you will be doing and how you'll do it. The elation of freedom should also be short-lived, unless you are a complete sloth – most of us actually need some routine in our lives, and the discipline of work, to keep our minds stimulated and our metabolisms in shape. If this seems fanciful, just think of all the apparently healthy people who retire and die very quickly afterwards: it's as if, once they lose the motivation of a job, their whole physical and mental infrastructure collapses. Work is a necessary evil, and not just because you need the money – it is a powerful stimulant that the average human actually requires.

Even if you're fortunate enough not to have gone through the process of redundancy, and have made an active decision to set up in business on your own – the 'pull' rather than the 'push' factor – you will still experience many of these emotions. The difference is that they will come in a slightly altered schedule: handing in your notice will provide a very temporary sense of elation, which will almost undoubtedly be followed by periods of deep depression and panic as you realize that things aren't going to be quite as straightforward as you imagined. And the people who make this active decision often feel some regret, wishing that they had not been so hasty and wondering if their old employer might take them back.

Whatever the order in which these emotions arrive, it's vital to accept them, deal with them, and then move on. Experienced sole traders learn to deal with the highs and lows of life on the open road, handling success and failure with equanimity. They become pragmatists, accepting that things don't always go as planned and adjusting their operation to take account of new circumstances. They suffer the frustrations of the small trader as part of the price they are willing to pay for freedom, and you must learn to deal with the slings and arrows in exactly the same way. If you let your emotions get in the way they will cloud your judgement and damage your business.

By one route or another you have now reached the stage where you need to be putting in some serious thought about what you will actually do to support yourself. In the following chapter we will deal with The Big Idea, and why the absence of one is not necessarily A Bad Thing.

Chapter Two

THE BIG IDEA

'If a man write a better book, preach a better sermon, or make a better mouse-trap than his neighbour, tho' he build his house in the woods, the world will make a beaten path to his door.'

Ralph Waldo Emerson

'There is no new thing under the sun.' Ecclesiastes

Everyone dreams of having the Big Idea. Big Ideas, it is commonly believed, make Big Money. And, whilst that may be true, they also normally need big money to turn them into marketable products and services. A genuinely new concept requires careful research to validate its feasibility, and research takes time and money to complete and interpret. Even the most comprehensive research is likely to provide, at best, empirical evidence about the viability of a new idea – in short, no-one really knows whether it will work until the customers vote with their feet and their wallets, either beating a path to your door or leaving you entangled in the undergrowth.

The Service is the Product

From personal experience, I can vouch for Ralph Waldo Emerson's advice, and you will find that most of the case studies in this book are concerned with people who have followed it. Successful entrepreneurs, in the main, have looked at an existing market and have identified a gap – maybe in service quality, or reliability, or price – and have worked to fill that gap, not by inventing a different product but by re-engineering an existing one so that it better satisfies customer requirements. When you fly on Virgin, you travel on the same type of aeroplane as British Airways uses, but you will find distinctly different service levels: neither can be categorically defined as 'better', but they are different. That is what marks out the successful business: there may well be a product that is largely a commodity, such as air travel or groceries, but the method by which it is delivered, the service, is where differentiation can make all the difference between profit and loss. The sole trader is wonderfully well positioned to understand client service requirements and translate them into 'the better mouse-trap'. Why?

Small is Beautiful

In the classic vertical organization, with different division heads in charge of sales, marketing, product development, research, operations and production, customer service, finance and admin-istration, there is very rarely anyone who has the total picture, the full story of how customers perceive their organization and why they choose to buy, or not to buy, their company's products. The sales force reports to a sales manager who reports to the sales director who reports to an executive vice-president, ad infinitum until you reach the chairman who is too busy calculating the value of his stock options to worry too much about the cus-tomers. Each division has similar reporting lines, with managers building personal fiefdoms and erecting barriers around their empire to repel attacks from other divisions. The poor old customer comes very low down on the list of priorities. But sole traders have no need to build these barrages between them, their clients and the markets they are trying to serve. They do not need to go through elaborate approval processes and endless research and analysis before deciding to tweak their service levels or change the product range: they have the flexibility to change, and to anticipate change, almost instantaneously. This is the key differentiating factor for the small business – it is an agile and enormously flexible animal. As if to prove the point, many big companies have recently decided that they need to break themselves up into smaller, more autonomous units, with less centralized control from HQ, so that they can react more quickly to changes in the market. Big companies want to be like small companies.

This principle, that businesses need to be closer to their customers and quicker to react to market changes, is becoming ingrained into our society, from the way we buy our food to the way we invest our money. Managers are working much harder to select the tier of customer they want to attract, and construct their marketing strategy accordingly. The same should be true for the sole trader: even before you have decided what exactly your product is going to be, you need to understand the target market in general terms. Are you looking for high-value, low-volume work, where you will rely on a few major contracts to earn your living, or do you want to supply a low-cost, no-frills service that attracts customers in their thousands? The service level you aim to provide is therefore critical to the design of your product, and must be determined at the outset. It is at this stage, when you're agonizing over the decision to go it alone, that you must draw up that favourite tool of the management consultants, the T-square.

Navel Contemplation

The T-square routine is both classic and simple. You take a blank piece of paper, and draw a line down the centre, heading the two resulting columns 'Strengths' and 'Weaknesses', or 'Advantages' and 'Disadvantages'. That's the easy part – filling it up, and making sure you have more pluses than minuses, will require harder work.

Intuitively, most of us think we know what our strengths and weaknesses are, but our own perceptions of ourselves are often pretty wide of the mark: you only need to listen to a tape-recording of your own voice to realize that others hear you very differently to the way you hear yourself, and the same is true of the image you project. When you sit down to analyse your good, and not so good, points, it's important to poll the opinion of others: what do they think about you, and what would they suggest as the best route for you to follow? When I was going through the process of this self-analysis, I believed that I was a good verbal communicator, and I set my sights on using that skill to earn my living, but the people I approached eventually taught me that I should concentrate on written communication. No one likes being told they're wrong but, if the money's there, you can learn to live with it!

The T-square of strengths and weaknesses is only of any value if you're brutally frank about yourself. We're not all brilliant at everything, but there is a demand for different skills and aptitudes, so the fact that you hate making customer presentations may not be a major burden if you're planning to deliver a service that can be bought on the phone or through the mail, for instance. You will have to adapt your strengths to make sure that the product and service don't require you to do things you feel uncomfortable with. Many of the people featured in the case studies could not be described as natural sales-people, but they have developed a strategy, and a service, that overcomes this problem – and we'll talk more about sales techniques later.

This process – of determining your own values and virtues – is fundamental to your future success. Before you have decided on how you will make your money, and with what, you must have a very clear idea of the type of person you are, and what attributes you can most effectively use to be successful. As a sole trader, you will be disproportionately reliant on your own character and culture for the success of your business – in effect, people will be buying you as much as the product. You become the service, so you must ensure that what you are selling can be satisfactorily serviced by you as an individual. Just as Marks & Spencer is associated with Quality, Service and Value, you must be associated with tangible benefits that your customers will want. We all know, from our experience of working in organizations, how much the corporate culture differs from company to company – how some are customer-driven, some are cost-driven, and some are driven by nothing – and the sole trader, although he or she may be sitting in the spare bedroom, has to develop a culture in exactly the same way as big businesses, which must be based on their character and what they are most comfortable with.

Service Comes First

So the Big Idea is not really about the product – what you sell – as it is about the service – how you sell it. It's important to realize that everyone in business has a product, even if you can't touch and feel it. Management consulting, interior decoration, book-keeping – these are all products, instantly recognizable as such by consumers – but they are simply categories in the *Yellow Pages*. 'I am a plumber' tells the customer something, but not enough to induce him to buy; 'I am a plumber with a 24-hour helpline and a guaranteed response time of 2 hours' tells him much more about the service that differentiates your product. In the following chapters we'll look at these 'Unique Selling Points' (USPs) in more detail; one of the most common failures of businesses is to develop these features as bolt-on extras to the product, regardless of whether they are perceived as useful by customers. 'I am plumber who only uses SupaStrength tools', for instance, says absolutely nothing useful to the average consumer of plumbing services. Customers don't care what tools you use, just as they really don't care what systems a bank uses to produce monthly statements: they're much more concerned that the statements are accurate, legible, delivered on time, and come in well-sealed envelopes. That is service, as opposed to product.

Assuming that your T-square has more pluses than minuses, you are now in a position to look at your proposed product. Whatever field you settle on, you face the prospect of going in blind. Very few of us have the luxury of knowing our market perfectly, with a guaranteed client base. For the vast majority, instinct and informal research are going to play the major roles in determining what we sell. We believe we know about a gap in the market; if we're very lucky, we may have been told by others that our feeling is correct. But proof of that hunch will only come when potential clients – 'suspects', you might call them – turn into prospects, and then start sending in signed contracts and, eventually, hard cash. The sad fact is, most customers are deeply suspicious of untried products, of things that are trying to break the mould – witness the Sinclair C5. Buyers are a conservative breed, and they want to be reassured that what they are buying, and the service wrapped around it, are based on something familiar. So your product doesn't have to be a mould-breaker; it just has to be delivered so that it's either better, cheaper, more reliable, or quicker than the competition.

Study the Winners

It follows, therefore, that you should study the competition carefully before embarking on your own venture. Sometimes this may be easy: you may yourself have been a buyer, or consumer, of similar products from competitors when you were with your former employer. You'll know how they delivered the product, and what you liked and disliked about it. But it's all too easy to draw conclusions from this experience that may be flawed, either because your own judgement is clouded by highly personal perceptions – the salesman suffered from acute halitosis, for example – or because the supplier has subsequently adapted their product and service to meet the objections that you have. If you assume that you are a reasonably rational human being, and that your buying priorities are not going to differ dramatically from those you wish to sell to, then you might be just as well off drawing up your own wish-list for the features and benefits of the product you want to deliver. Ask yourself the question: 'If I were buying this product, what would I be looking for that would make me buy it?' What makes you shop in Sainsbury's rather than Tesco? Is it convenience, price, range of goods, service, opening hours? How do you, as a consumer, make these buying decisions? Remind yourself that you are an expert in the field you've decided to concentrate on – so you must have the answers to these questions before you can design your product and service. Whatever you're going to sell, people must want to buy it – and they'll need solid reasons to do so.

As you study the competition, you may reach the conclusion that you cannot offer anything that they're not already supplying. Usually, this is a mistake. We don't all buy the same brand of toothpaste, or drive the same cars, irrespective of whether they have what appear to be exactly the same features and benefits. You can get far too concerned about what the competition is, or might be, doing, and end up in a state of paralysis as you try to work out a new twist or additional bells and whistles. If you have a good product, and can back it up with good service, people will buy it. In the same way as buyers' irrationality can work against you – they simply won't choose you, in spite of your obvious advantages – it can also work in your favour. Perhaps people will use you simply because they like you, or because they are already giving too much business to another supplier and want to spread their exposure. Buyers are driven not only by sensible, logical and identifiable criteria, but also by a host of other considerations that you may never see or hear of. What you must do is ensure that you are an entirely credible alternative to their current suppliers.

Value, not Price

In this highly complex equation of buyers' needs and wants, it will undoubtedly be the case that you lose most sleep over price. It is the natural inclination of most sole traders to assume that they will have to be cheaper than established competitors to stand any chance of success. But go back to the association of M & S with the three words 'Quality, Service, Value' – notice how the first two words say nothing about the cost of their products, and the last one is 'value' rather than 'price'. A cynic is 'the man who knows the price of everything and the value of nothing,' said Oscar Wilde, and cynics you do not need as customers. In a later chapter we will deal with how to price your products but, in the first days of your new life as a sole trader, you should already have a good idea of how important price will be in your overall mix of service. To many buyers, price is synonymous with quality: the higher the price, the better the quality. When we visit the supermarket and look at two tins of baked beans, one branded and one own-label, the former more expensive than the latter, we subconsciously conclude that the branded product costs more because there is something about it that is different – better – than the cheaper one. This may well be utterly the wrong conclusion, but the point is worth bearing in mind.

In fact, pricing is as much a function of determining your own worth as it is about recovering your costs and making a profit. When you go into business for yourself, you need to have a belief in yourself, and your ability to deliver a product that someone wants. That conviction, that you will be adding value to your customers, has to be unshakeable, however queasy you may feel. It is only when you can put your hand on your heart and say: 'I'm worth what I'm charging', that you will start winning business. Those who shy away from this commitment will soon discover that 'cheap' equals 'tacky', and people don't want to buy tacky products – and if you want to sell them, then this book is not for you. The beauty of pricing as a sole trader is that you have no constraints: you're not going to print a glossy brochure which locks you into product prices for a year or more, nor are you going to be forced to keep your prices low if the business goes well and you realize that you could charge more. But your starting point must be that you have something of value – yourself, your know-how, your skills, your reliability – which commands and deserves a fair price, regardless of what your competitors are charging.

By this stage, you should have formulated the strategy for your business: you have made the decision to go it alone, you have done your T-square and have determined the key strengths that you have which will help to win business, and you know what you're going to sell. The good news is that this is absolutely vital in planning your future. The bad news is, that is the easy part. Translating all this navel-gazing into real money is substantially more difficult, but much more rewarding.

Chapter Three

FIRST STEPS

Starting your own business is exhilarating. The freedom to manage your own life is most addictive, allowing you to dream extensively, setting your sights wherever you wish. But this freedom is also dangerous: the absence of any guiding hand to tell you what to do, and when to do it, is probably the most difficult aspect of being a sole trader. Suddenly there is no discipline, no routine, no deadlines and, most dangerously, no sense of time management. Many former wage slaves have discovered to their cost that they simply cannot function unless someone else is calling the shots, establishing a regime and framework for gainful employment. Of course, should you become a great success as a sole trader, you will always have that discipline, because it will be determined by customers. But the early days of the self-employed can be disorienting, as you struggle to come to terms with all that excess time and space.

Time is of the Essence

With almost everyone who decides to work for themselves, there will be a very uncomfortable first period during which there is no business. This period can be the death of the budding sole trader. What is absolutely critical during the early days is to establish a routine, and stick to it. It doesn't really matter what the routine is, and it must be one that you are most happy with. The sole trader doesn't have to work between nine and five: most of us end up working much longer hours than that, but the timing of your work should be structured effectively to meet the current and future requirements of your business.

Nine to five is, however, an extremely important period of the day, because that is when your potential and existing customers are most likely to want to deal with you. Your day must be built around that requirement. So time management must take account of all the critical hours in the day, and all the other time when less vital functions can be performed. This book, for instance, was largely written between the hours of six and nine o'clock in the morning. The phone doesn't ring, and the mail hasn't arrived, so there are few distractions and fewer excuses for not getting on with it. But the standard working day must be sacrosanct, set aside exclusively for servicing existing customers and developing a list of suspects and prospects. Everything else is subsidiary to this objective: the bank manager, tax man, utility company and accountant don't care at what time of day you handle your correspondence with them, so deal with it when your customers aren't likely to demand something from you.

Avoid the Administrivia

But ... when there are no customers, what do you do? The temptation in your first days will be to concern yourself with things that really don't contribute anything at all to the future well-being and profitability of your business. Remember the advice of that man from the Department of Employment: nothing else matters except bringing in live, paying customers. Customers don't materialize unless you go out and talk to them, make them aware of what you're selling and why they should buy it. Spending time with a printer, designing embossed stationery with a fancy logo on laid vellum paper, only achieves one thing: additional, unnecessary expenditure.

When I first went on the road, one of the questions I was most frequently asked was: 'Are you working from home?'

Initially, this worried me. Was I sending the wrong message by setting up my business in the spare bedroom? Should I have an office with a good address and secretarial facilities? But these people weren't concerned about that: they wanted to know a little bit about me, and how I would operate. In fact, having my business at home was seen as an advantage: I was keeping my overheads low, which would translate into lower pricing, and I was focusing on the key issue of winning new customers. If I did that successfully, then I'd think about getting an office. Even the stationery was printed on my own PC. I installed a separate phone line and good answering and fax machines, and that was enough.

We're all guilty of getting obsessed with what I call the 'administrivia' of running a business. From our days as employees, we're so used to having all the trappings of big business that we cannot conceive of the fact that they simply don't matter. As soon as you've set up your operation, your name and address are passed to a hundred companies trying to sell you everything from stationery to conferences to software, and they're all very good at marketing. They want you to believe that you cannot function effectively unless you have their product, that you won't be taken seriously unless you have all their wonderful goods. But being a sole trader doesn't work like that. You don't have to feel apologetic about keeping your costs under control and relying on your products and service to win and retain business. The image you project is clearly important, but you should never forget that your customers are buying you, not your image. You are the best representative of what you are selling. Naturally, your correspondence with clients must look professional, and you must be able to handle phone enquiries effectively and efficiently. So always check the spelling and grammar of anything that leaves your desk in an envelope, and install separate phone lines and call-waiting services and fax machines: these are all much cheaper than renting redundant office space that is used primarily for storage and a place to hang your coat.

Outsource the Trivia

The other point to bear in mind is that, just as people will often turn to you for help with things that they'd rather not do themselves, you should look for help with anything that you don't feel entirely comfortable with, or that isn't adding value to your business. Outsourcing is another management buzz word, but it makes a lot of sense. There are plenty of examples of how outsourcing can be used effectively. Take the case of mailshots, which are essential for most fledgling businesses. There is a huge industry in mailing lists: list brokers spend tedious and agonizing hours compiling lists of potential targets, and can deliver them to you on diskette or in label format. Many will also handle the mailshot for you, stuffing envelopes and sending them out at their reduced postage cost. Do you really want to handle this yourself? Imagine the amount of time it would take you to replicate their service, and then work out how much lost time, time that could be spent with customers, you would incur. List brokers work on this basis, and charge accordingly. They know that they have to beat your internal costs and sell the 'hassle factor', so they are almost always cost-effective. Similarly, the Royal Mail tries very hard to make your life easier. They offer a tremendous range of services to make mailshots cheaper and easier to fulfil. Do you want to lick five hundred stamps at a go? You don't have to – the Royal Mail will do it for you.

Accounting for Success

Of all the services that cry out to be outsourced, accounting is the most important. If, like me, you are hopeless at managing your own finances, an accountant is absolutely essential. Every year my accountant saves me more money than he charges – by a substantial margin. Good accountants are literally worth their weight in gold. You pay them for their expertise – expertise that most of us don't have. They know about income tax, financing,

National Insurance, VAT and cashflow management. Don't confuse their services with those of book-keepers, who will make sure that all the debits and credits end up in the right place. Keeping your own books is actually very simple nowadays: you can buy a software package for less than fifty pounds, and it won't let you make a mess of things. But the accountant can help you to take full advantage of all the allowances to which you're entitled, guiding you through an increasingly complex maze of regulation, and I believe that one should be hired as soon as you start out.

Absolute Bankers

Earlier in the book I suggested that any pay-off you get from a former employer should be set aside and left untouched. When you are starting from point zero, it concentrates the mind wonderfully. You very quickly realize that, if you don't work, you don't eat. No longer can you afford to take the day off if you're suffering from a hangover or don't feel in quite the right mood. Finance – more specifically, the lack of it – will nag away at you, and cashflow management is, more often than not, the single largest contributory factor to failure. You can be highly successful in what you do, but if cash doesn't arrive when it should, you can collapse under the burden of your operating costs. Thinking about money, and planning for how things will actually turn out – as opposed to how they should turn out in the perfect world of most self-help books – is essential in your early planning stages.

For most of us, contact with a clearing bank is limited to our personal lives: we have a current account, a salary is paid in and we spend it (and more besides, in many cases). Few of us have had dealings with our bank on a business level, but all that changes when you set up on your own. If your bank is as unsympathetic as most I know, then you will have a very hard struggle to convince them that they should take you seriously as a business customer. Sure, they will open a business account for you, and may give you an incentive to do so by waiving charges for an initial period. But much of the noise made by the UK clearing banks about their support for the self-employed is no more than marketing bluster promulgated from a head-office department that has never seen the sharp end of life. Your local branch will probably only have one consideration – what money is going to come in to the account? The old saw about banks only lending money to people who don't need it is painfully near to the truth when it comes to sole traders.

Why do you need to convince your bank of your professionalism and the soundness of your business plan? Essentially, there are two reasons. Firstly, changing your status from salaried employee to sole trader will start the alarm bells ringing in your local branch. If you have overdraft facilities, you can expect them to be, at the very least, reviewed, and quite possibly cancelled or substantially reduced. Quite naturally, the banks consider sole traders to represent a greater credit risk. Whilst this is natural, it is also typically short-sighted. Sole traders have an infinite opportunity to make money. Salaried employees remain on a fixed income, which may edge up year-on-year but will never offer the same potential for serious wealth. Not all sole traders remain that way: many go on and grow to become fantastically successful companies. But the banks don't all see it like that. They mostly look for security, and they'll search for it everywhere – can they take a charge on your house? Will you deposit your redundancy cheque with them in a special account as collateral? What other assets do you have? These requests are to be resisted. Although legally you may well be synonymous with your business, it is very important to draw a practical distinction between the two.

The Art of the Forecast

To counter this, you need to start behaving like a professional business person from the moment you decide to go it alone. This, unfortunately, means that you have to prepare a business plan and cash-flow forecasts. There have been numerous rainforests decimated by publishers in order to bring you lots of information and advice on how to compile these, and I do not intend to contribute further to global de-forestation by recycling that data. Business plans and cashflow forecasts are useful only in as much as they are believed by other people. It is crass to think that, on day one of your new life as a micro-entrepreneur, you can have even the faintest notion of where you'll be in six months' time, and yet any banker worth their salt will ask you to predict exactly this. So you must have a plan, based on whatever criteria you feel are most important for your audience, and you must be able to present it professionally and confidently, even if it is totally without foundation. I'm not suggesting that you lie, but remember that forecasts are only forecasts. If the Chancellor of the Exchequer was fired every time the Treasury got a forecast wrong, we'd soon run out of MPs to do the job.

Opinion is sharply divided about the merits of cashflow forecasts. Some sole traders diligently do and re-do their forecasts, amending them in the light of experience. Others – and I fall into this category – consider them to be a complete waste of time. Customers don't bring business to you when you're expecting them to, and they don't pay their bills when you want them to. As that covers the inflows side of the forecast, you can only reasonably predict when you'll need to pay money out – and that, of course, is entirely dependent on when money comes in to meet your obligations. But you have to accept that banks like to see numbers on charts, and have it all explained to them.

Professional Behaviour

Your personal and your business lives should not be intertwined. If you use a room in your house as your office, you may be able to claim a portion of your running costs against your total tax liability. If the taxman recognizes that there are two separate parts to your life, even under the same roof, then so should you. You should establish a separate business account, and put all income and expenditure related to the business through it. Where you pay for business expenses out of your own pocket, this must show up as a loan from you to the business in your books. Banks have difficulty understanding this, and they tend to patronize you as a result, as if you were playing at running a business. But once you get to the stage where they will only continue to lend you money if you put up personal assets as security, you should seriously consider alternative methods of finance.

Funding Failure?

The question then arises – why do you need finance? For a lot of sole traders, business can start with a minimum of capital. It's worth bearing in mind that a lot of items – fax machines, PCs, phones, even office furniture – can be rented. This has a very positive effect on cash flow, even though it may not make economic sense in the long term. But the major reason for finance is what you might call 'gap management' – plugging the gap between anticipated receipts and expenses. You are going to need to maintain very good relationships with all your suppliers, so their invoices have to be paid on time. You cannot afford to behave like a big company and take a cavalier attitude towards payables. Word soon gets around that you're a bad credit risk, and that is a black spot that takes a long time to erase. Bills have to be paid but money may not come in at the same time. For most of us, this is when short-term finance is needed, and this is when the bank should be used. If you have established at the outset that you are running a good business, and your bank manager has seen steady earnings and prudent management, you're much more likely to get help. But what happens if you don't?

Again, there appear to be two schools of thought on this. The first subscribes to what I would term as the Mr Micawber management theory – 'something will turn up'. Those who sign up to this are eternal optimists – and there is nothing intrinsically wrong with that – but it is hardly a good way to manage your money. Possibly the toughest discipline of all for the sole trader is to put money aside for contingencies, either real or potential. If you earn well in excess of your costs, it is only too tempting to spend that profit – on new or better equipment, or a car, or a good holiday that you thoroughly deserve. But money spent is money spent – I well remember having to sell a nice little car that I'd bought for my wife in order to pay the VAT one quarter. Saving, especially in the early days, is tough, but it brings its rewards later. The second, more prudent theory suggests that you should reserve for everything, and leave that money untouched. Good as that may sound, it is incredibly hard advice to follow. The best approach is probably somewhere in the middle: you should put excess money to one side, but you should use it if you can really convince yourself, and your family, that spending it will be a good investment or that there is no other alternative.

Borrowing money to service overheads should be against the law. Essentially, if you cannot finance your activities through cashflow, there is something fundamentally wrong with your business. Perhaps you should be considering a different structure, with shareholders or venture capitalists, if your business is capital-intensive. Or perhaps you have simply misread the market – and borrowing to continue trading is the worst thing you can do. Overheads must fit in with actual, rather than anticipated, income – and fixed overheads are the worst of all. That's why you shouldn't rent office space, the price of which doesn't change according to your income, or take on other major commitments that are fixed and difficult to get out of.

Cutting Commitments

Such commitments might include life-assurance and pension premiums, as well as private health-care plans. When you are an employee, a lot of these things may come as part of the total compensation package. It is only when you enter the real world, where you have to pay for these things yourself, that you realize just how valuable these benefits are. Pension provision, in particular, is extremely expensive unless you are planning to retire to Bombay. Fortunately, some of the more enlightened pension houses have designed special self-employed schemes that have a flexible payment arrangement, meaning that you pay in only what you can afford. Believe me, there will be many months when you think that is zero, but bear in mind that you get assistance from the taxman with pension payments qualifying as an allowable expense. The problem is, once you've put the money in you cannot get it out again.

Assurance and insurance are also difficult to deal with. If you have dependants, you must obviously be covered for death, but should you also have serious illness cover? And is private health insurance absolutely necessary? We still have the best national health service in the world and, if you're really sick, they look after you pretty well. What you must plan for is what will happen if your ability to earn money is inhibited for whatever reason: the self-employed do not get sick pay, and it therefore makes sense to cover yourself for all eventualities. There are many schemes that are reasonably cost-effective; bear in mind, however, that cover for new sole traders will probably be in the form of a cash lump sum, because neither the insurer nor you can estimate what your monthly earnings will be.

Another shock to the system is the car. If you've been used to a brand-new company car every three or four years, with insurance and maintenance paid for by your grateful employer, you are in for a rude awakening. Car insurance is phenomenally expensive, as is servicing. The problem is, you get accustomed to the luxuries of a modern car quite easily, and there is no doubt that we Brits are tremendously conscious of the status a car bestows upon us. Buying a second-hand car with 90,000 on the clock and no service history is oddly unappealing for most of us. But you have to keep your outgoings low, and most cars nowadays last a long time. Steel yourself for a major cultural adjustment when you hand back the keys to your sleek executive limo and swap it for a slightly battered banger. Be prepared to write off the cost of the car over a maximum of two years, and look at it as a method of transport rather than a talisman of your achievements. You'll soon get used to it, I promise you.

Budgetary Control

Perhaps you have now discerned that there is a difference between what you tell the outside world about your finances and what really goes on. The annual accounts that you and your accountant draw up are merely a snapshot of a year's activity: they say nothing about the roller-coaster of cashflow during those 12 months, nothing about what will happen in the future or what has already happened since you signed off on them. Essentially, there is also a major difference between forecasts and budgets and, without wanting to get too technical and out of your and my depth, it is important that you recognize the difference. Forecasts and plans are what you might be willing to show to other people, like your bank manager. They make predictions about the future health of the business. Budgets, however, are for your consumption alone. I hate to tell you this, but budgets are a big deal when you're in business for yourself.

Budgeting is a process most of us go through in our personal lives, even if it is in the most dilatory and half-hearted fashion. We allocate our known income to cover all the known expenses, whether on a monthly or weekly basis, and most of us manage to live just within, or only marginally beyond, our means. For the sole trader, budgeting is just as important, and obviously becomes intertwined with our personal finances. As an employee money is coming in on a regular basis – maybe not as much as we'd like or we think we deserve – so the process is, to some extent, made easier. But the self-employed rarely enjoy that luxury, so both sides of the equation are based on forecasts. The difference between a forecast and a budget is that the latter is based on the 'zero-option' strategy: I start with nothing, so how am I going to live? The budget is the one part of your financial management process that you should pay daily attention to: what money has come in today, and what bills have to be paid? If you leave this to chance you will end up in an almighty mess. You have to know how much you need to spend to keep the business going, what your withdrawals will be to satisfy your personal commit-ments, and where and when you most realistically expect the money to come from. What you tell other people does not include this micro-analysis of your cashflow, where each day's activity represents more experience about how you will manage your cash.

To avoid the danger of unpaid bills piling up in a mountain with no means of paying them, you must anticipate your total cash needs and budget for them. Go through your personal bank statements for the last 12 months and pull out all the debits, standing orders and other regular payments. Look at them carefully and see if any can be cut, just like any Tory Chancellor would do. Then calculate what you actually spend every year, and determine what you might be able to live on for the next 12 months. Once you've sorted out your personal finances, the job becomes more difficult, because you simply have no experience of life as a sole trader. But there are expenditures that you know will occur: the phone bill will go up, as might domestic heat and light if you're working from home. What will the cost of goods sold be? How much will I need to spend on stationery and postage? Will I need to join a trade association, and how much will the subscription be? What should my allowance be for trade journals and newspapers? Should I buy better software for my

PC? Keep on adding to the list of expenses that you might incur, and draw up different scenarios, the 'what if' analysis that will tell you how to behave if things go better or worse than planned. When you have finally arrived at a gross expenditure figure, that is merely the beginning of the budget process, because everything will change in the light of experience. But you need to have a good idea of what the total cost of your operation, both from a business and personal perspective, will be, and you'll want to carry that figure around with you whilst you're trying to earn enough money to cover it. Budgets are just as much of a moving target as forecasts, but they are the tools by which you will manage your finances. If you don't work to a budget you will never gain control of your money and, however profitable the business is, you'll always suffer from cashflow problems.

By now you've probably realized that planning for success is, for the most part, laborious, demoralizing and time-consuming. But it soon passes, and the agony decreases as you start out on the really exciting part – taking your idea to the great unwashed and finding out if you're ever going to make any money.

Chapter Four

GO FORTH
AND MULTIPLY

Selling is what other people do. Life assurance and double-glazing: these products need salespeople, men and women who will sit in your home drinking coffee until midnight in the hope that you'll finally collapse from exhaustion and sign the contract just to get them out of your house. Selling, according to the British, is slightly odious, a job not considered as a profession, not what your parents had in mind for you as they guided you through your formative years.

But selling is a skill, requiring stamina, expertise, patience and durability. For most of us, the idea of selling ourselves, or the products that represent us, is more than a little disturbing. We don't like the concept of having to extol our own virtues, make promises about what we can deliver and why it will benefit our prospective customers. We have a natural reticence, an immovable modesty, about our own strengths, and believe that, if we start talking about them too loudly, people will think we are boasting, big-headed egomaniacs.

Best Sellers

The best salespeople don't sell; they let their customers buy. They present an irrefutable list of reasons – features *and* benefits – why the client should buy the product, and they always ask for the business. They don't sulk when they don't win a new customer; they learn from the experience, and use that knowledge when it comes to the next prospect. And they never forget people who've said no in the past; they come back to them at a later stage, maybe with news of a new twist in the product or service, maybe just to keep their name in the customer's mind. They know that buyers' criteria change, and that they may become dissatisfied with their existing supplier, so they don't give up: they just regroup.

The best sellers work to turn themselves into consultants: as the saying goes, they have two ears and only one mouth, so they use them in that proportion. They listen to buyer requirements, and try to adapt the product and service features to meet those needs, translating features into benefits. They want to become partners, rather than suppliers or vendors, and they know that the best way to do this is by understanding what the customer wants, and then sell them exactly that. They also know that a satisfied customer comes back for more: evidence suggests that it is five times more expensive to win a new client than it is to get additional business from an existing one.

Raising Awareness

I can hear you saying: 'This is all very well, but what has that got to do with me? You're talking about professional salespeople with a large support staff; I'm just a sole trader. If my product is good enough, it'll sell itself.' And yes, for 0.0001 per cent of products, you would be right. But, if you have accepted Ecclesiates' argument that there is nothing new under the sun, and your product is aiming to do something evolutionary, rather than something revolutionary, then you'll need to sell it. Most sole traders very rapidly realize that, however brilliant their idea is, people will not beat a path to their door if they don't know where the door is. Selling is all about awareness: buyers must be aware that your product is out there, just screaming to be bought. This doesn't mean grand advertising schemes, or mass mailshots;

it simply means getting your name onto the buyers' shortlist of potential suppliers.

Product Positioning

Let's consider the word marketing, which many people confuse with sales. In fact, the British, if they have to be involved in sales, often like to refer to it as marketing: it has a more professional sound to it, and dissociates the activity from the high-pressure antics of those double-glazing wideboys. Marketing is really concerned with product positioning and awareness, through the use of all the techniques like advertising, sponsorship, press coverage, etc., whilst sales is concerned with only one thing – getting the business. Salespeople use the market awareness of their product, through the marketing efforts, to get in front of potential customers. But for sole traders, sales and marketing are going to be rolled into one function, and that function rests entirely with us. It doesn't matter what you call it, as long as it results in the primary objective of every business – getting paying customers.

As part of the process of positioning, you should analyse yourself, your product, and the market in which you plan to operate (including your competitors). Typically, this analysis takes the form of a SWOT evaluation – Strengths, Weaknesses, Opportunities and Threats – so that you consider each aspect of ths business and its position in relation to your aspirations.

When you have drawn up your SWOT analysis, and have concluded that there is a need for your product, you should start worrying about how this need will be satisfied. Before thinking about this, you need to be sure that what you are going to sell can be sold. This sounds intuitive, but great ideas are often impossible to turn into reality – and hard cash. If your product is simple, selling it won't present much of a problem; but sole traders often sell a service rather than a product – interior design and management consulting, for instance – where there is no underlying 'hard' product. How do you sell something that is intangible, that is differentiated merely by the service attached to it?

Price as a Driver

The natural conclusion of many sole traders is to assume that price will be the driver. Only the most confident of us can start out in business with the complete conviction that what we are selling is so good, so compelling, that buyers will pay any price to acquire it. For most of us, we want to undercut the competition, which may be represented by bigger, fatter businesses with higher overheads but a stable customer base. If we aim low, the thinking goes, we are likelier to hit the target. But pricing is only one factor in the equation and, if you start at the lowest possible price, you will always struggle to raise it to more profitable levels later. You don't want to set a precedent for cheapness – if anything, you should never use the word cheap (try saying it to yourself a few times – it sounds horrid!). 'Cost-effective' or 'good value' are much better ways of describing what you have to offer.

Who are my Customers?

So the SWOT analysis should be accompanied by another chart: features and benefits. I've already discussed the problems of having product features to which no discernible benefits are attached. Features are only important if they can be identified as having a benefit to your customer. And different customers have different needs: you cannot classify clients as a homogeneous group, all seeking the same service levels and product features. In the US, product manufacturers work very closely with retailers to discover exactly what each shopper buys, so that they can understand how to sell more of the right product to that consumer. If the majority of consumers have dishwashers, for example, they need to find out who buys powder and who buys liquid. They need to know if they buy scouring pads and other items that suggest they also do hand-washing of certain items. Even amongst dishwasher-owners, there are differing levels of user, and the product manufacturers want to target their sales promotion campaigns to each level.

In exactly the same way, you will need to think about the different classes of buyer that you want to serve. If you are going into business as an interior designer, you could target your service at many different buyers: you could concentrate on supplying the retail end of the business – people who are actually going to live in the homes you design – or you could attack the wholesale end of the market, serving property developers and builders. There are numerous permutations in between, all of which will offer you opportunities. And most of those permutations only become evident once you've started in business.

Where to Begin?

So how do you get your message across? You've had your idea, you've done your analysis, thought of a snappy name for your business, got a free entry from *Yellow Pages*, and you're ready to go out there and knock 'em dead. But the phone won't be ringing off the hook. You need to do some marketing first. And, as every successful micro-entrepreneur will tell you, your first customers will almost always be people who already know you. How many times have we read in the business pages of the press that a senior manager has left a company but will continue to act as a consultant for them? That's an obvious place to start for many of us – with our former employer or, better still, with its customers or competitors. When you leave a company, you leave a gap. You were – I hope! – performing some function that was important to them, and now it has gone, as have the skills and expertise associated with it. You've taken something away that they needed, and were prepared to pay you for. This is an incredibly difficult lesson to learn, for two reasons.

Firstly, you probably feel some residual ill-will towards your former employer, whether justified or not. Perhaps they made you redundant, which never helps to cement goodwill. Perhaps you left voluntarily because you were fed up with the way you were being treated. Either way, you're not going to be mad keen to go back to them and try and sell something to them. You may be worried that they won't take you seriously. But they do know you, and they do have a good idea of your strengths and weaknesses, quite possibly to a greater degree than you do. And all companies are looking at ways to save money: if they believe that you could do something for them, without them having to pay your National Insurance and other benefits, they might just be tempted to use you. What's the worst thing that could happen to you if you go back to your former employer and ask for some business? They can say no – and then you've ruled them out as customers. But they might say yes.

Secondly, most of us tend to undervalue ourselves. Initially, this manifests itself in the way we think about pricing our services. But it also makes us wary of going out and selling ourselves, especially to people who have known us under different circumstances – especially the employer/employee relationship. Perhaps a personal anecdote is the best way of illustrating the point. About a year after I'd started in business, an old colleague of mine got in touch and said he needed help with a project he was running. I'd left the company he still worked for some three years before, but there were plenty of people there who knew me, and quite a few of them didn't like me (I was always hopeless at office politics!). He and I agreed the scope of the work, and we agreed on a price. He said he needed to run it past some of his managers, one of whom I'd worked for and who wasn't overly keen on the idea. But, as I pointed out when I met him, we weren't talking about the past. We were talking about how his needs would best be met, and about the skills that I could bring to the project. It was tough, but I got the contract, and it all worked out very positively. I didn't enjoy negotiating the deal, but the pay-off was worth it. And I learnt a very valuable lesson: sensible business managers will listen to a well-reasoned argument, and will put personal feelings to one side if they believe they will gain some competitive advantage by buying a service, regardless of the supplier.

If it's satisfying to win business from your former boss, how much sweeter it is to take business away from them! This is a well-trodden path – just look at the constant re-formation of the advertising business, where executives regularly jump ship and found new agencies with long names in the belief that they can pinch some valuable accounts from their ex-agency. If you have had anything to do with customers of your employer, you're incredibly well-positioned to go to them and sell whatever it is you're now doing. After all, if you were any good at your job, you'll have vital knowledge of how these customers operate, who the decision-makers are, and what buying criteria they use.

Competitors of your former employer also represent an excellent target market, although you have to very careful about how you sell to them – you don't want to end up in court. But, as long as the terms of your contract (or severance) don't restrict you from taking your expertise to the competition, you have a marvellous opportunity of immediately translating your knowledge and experience into a saleable commodity. My first three contracts came from exactly this source when I set up on my own. I carried immediate credibility within the industry, and people were keen to capitalize on my experience to learn more about how they should be running their operation. I didn't give away any trade secrets – remember that your knowledge of what your former employer does becomes stale the moment you walk out of the front door for the last time – but I brought a different perspective to my new customers.

Networks Work!

What I'm getting at is that the best bits of business, at least in the early days, come from existing contacts. The buzz word is networking. Horrible as it may seem, you have to accept that your top priority is business. You have to change people's perception of you – including your family, friends, acquaintances, colleagues – so that they realize that you are serious about your business. Life-assurance salesmen are past masters at this: they pick up huge amounts of business from the people they know. They network infinitely. So must you. Although it may sound incredibly unscientific, a lot of your business is going to come from word of mouth, people who know you telling other people they know about you. In a sense, it's the old-boy network in microcosm – 'I know a man who knows a man who could do something for you' – and, regardless of how the management gurus might want the economy to be run, this is what actually happens.

Think about it from the buyer's perspective, from your own experience as a buyer. You want your roof renovated. Do you look in the *Yellow Pages* and pick out three builders you've never heard of? Of course not: you ask people you know who've had their roofs done, and find out who is trustworthy. When you buy a car, you talk to other car-owners about their cars, and what they like and dislike. You don't pay much attention to the advertising and glossy brochures, as they are only telling you that the manufacturer is in business. They are making you aware of their products, but they can't tell you about the service. Other buyers can.

Networking is all about timing. I've lost count of the number of times I've made a call to someone whose name was given to me by a friend, and I've got the response: 'It's funny you should call, because I've just been thinking about how we could deal with this.' It doesn't always work like that, and many of your calls will bear no fruit immediately, but you should persevere. It's the hardest thing in the world to make a cold call on someone you've never met, and explain why you've got something they want – but once it's been successful, it's the most rewarding experience in the world. Never underestimate the power of networking: it can lead you into very profitable relationships with customers whom you might otherwise never reach.

The Message and the Medium

Networking is a powerful weapon in your sales and marketing armoury – but it is by no means the only one. When you're sitting alone in your converted attic, and wondering how to go about getting your message to the great unwashed, you have to be bold. I like the story about the school my children go to. The headmaster is the same age as me, but considerably more charismatic and dynamic. He left a large London school to set up on his own, a bold move at the end of the 80s when private education was being squeezed by the recession. He took a few pupils with him, but not nearly enough to make the school economically viable. He rented a church hall in Wimbledon, and he did everything himself – headmaster, janitor, cook, bursar and, most importantly, publicist. His educational beliefs were radical, and very attractive to the audience he wanted to reach, but he needed to get their attention. In the evenings, he would go round houses in the area and pop a flyer through the front door, explaining the values and principles of the school. But his master-stroke, in my opinion, was to get the national press interested. To them, he was an interesting case: initially, they were fascinated by the fact that he cooked the lunches himself but, once he'd hooked them, he could put his more important message across to a very wide audience. We read one of the articles and were intrigued; we went to see him, and immediately moved our boys there. He had communicated with us through an unconventional channel, very successfully and at very little cost to himself – brilliant marketing.

Similarly, you must be a relentless self-publicist. As in the case of the school, you must look at all possible ways of getting your message to the buying public. The press, for example, loves a good story about someone making it on their own, in an unconventional way. Newspaper articles are free publicity. If you can establish yourself as something of an expert on your subject, they'll always come to you for a quote or information. Journalists are lazy, and if they think they can get you to do their work for them, they will. Use that to your advantage. But there are other media that you should consider. That headmaster used flyers, and I know he got pupils as a result. I've bought services on the strength of a flyer, and I'm sure you have as well – if only a pizza delivered to your door. If they are informative, and identify a need in the reader, business may well result.

But flyers are not always appropriate, especially if you're not selling to the retail sector. If you need to reach other businesses, you need more sophisticated communications channels. And here we come to one of the big dangers that all sole traders face, a danger that can cripple you if you let it get out of control. I've already talked about the paralysis that can result from too much attention to the administrivia of business – the letterheads, the premises, and all the attendant peripheral activity – and marketing gives you ample scope to spend too much time and money for your own good. You think you need a brochure, perhaps, or some other marketing materials that establish your credentials and that must be printed to a high quality. You want to advertise in a trade magazine. You want to sponsor a stand at an exhibition. There are so many ways to spend your money, before you've even started earning any. You can justify this, you say to yourself, because it is an investment in the business – and therefore tax-deductible.

Research-based Selling

But you won't be paying any tax if you don't have any income. And brochures, however glossy, don't generate income. Selling does. There is no substitute for face-to-face communications. Make this your first priority – in fact, make it your only priority. You must get out and get recognized. To do that, you need to put in some heavy research. You need to know who to talk to, who to call; you need to know about your potential customers, those suspects who might become prospects. You'll already have some idea of this through your initial networking, and the contacts you've built up as an employee. But you need to supplement this with other sources of data on your suspect list.

How you go about this largely depends on the type of product and service you are selling. If you have a high-value product, to be sold to a relatively small group of customers, you are probably looking at a specialist market. That can be easy to get to – list brokers can often provide you with names, addresses and phone numbers of relevant contacts, for a fraction of the cost of putting the information together yourself. But if your product has broader appeal – like book-keeping services, or interior design – you'll need to think about other ways to reach the intended audience. Flyers come into their own with this type of market, either pushed through the letterbox or folded into the local newspaper. Don't forget the power of related marketing, too. If you are an interior designer, for example, you might be able to strike a deal with a local shop supplying material, leaving your business cards on the counter or displaying an advertisement in their shop window.

However you attack your chosen market, it will have to be a two-pronged approach. You need an awareness campaign, and you need to be selling yourself and your products. Too many people, from the largest business to the smallest concern, forget that both are important. Reliance on one will result in failure. You should have learnt this from your own experience as a buyer:

how often have you been impressed with an advertising campaign, only to find that the sales process leaves a lot to be desired? Banks and insurance companies have much to answer for: they spend massive amounts on creative advertising, only to disappoint their potential customers when it comes to product delivery. That is true for too many businesses: they over-promise and under-deliver. Anyone who has watched the advertisements for InterCity train services knows just how divorced from reality the advertising agency is: have you ever tried to play chess on a train?

We're now getting to the stage where you actually have to call on potential customers and sell yourself – yes, yourself. For most sole traders, the product is much less important than the service, and the service is entirely dependent upon you. You have to be trustworthy, dependable, honest, acceptable, and many other things, if the buyer is to select you. If you can't project that image, you're going to find things very tough. In the next chapter, we look at selling techniques for the sole trader: 99 per cent is common sense, but who has a premium on that?

Chapter Five

PAYING PUNTERS

There you are, sitting at your desk, your PC blinking at you, the phone strategically placed for quick access. Curiously, it isn't ringing. This is strange because you've followed all the advice in the previous chapters of this book, and yet there is still no sign of a customer.

One of the sadder side-effects of a free-market economy is that customers have a choice. There is almost nothing left in this country that is provided by a monopoly supplier. This may be good news for the advertising agencies, but it is very bad news for you. You have entered the competitive world of commerce and, however much you may dislike it, you have to compete like crazy to win business. Of course, you're going to compete on price and service and product benefits, but that won't be enough. For your small voice to be heard amongst the chorus of suppliers, you must get in front of customers and tell them why they need you. The fact that you already have a hundred good reasons for people to buy from you isn't enough: you have to communicate these to your chosen audience.

Warm Selling

Cold calling is something that nobody likes. Anyone that tells you otherwise is a liar. And cold calling is something that can be avoided, if you know how. In the previous chapter we looked at networking as a way of avoiding cold calling – using old contacts and friends of friends to effect an introduction – and this can often give you the kick-start you need. The most daunting task of all, however, is not the actual phone call to introduce yourself. That may well require the application of extra layers of deodorant, but it is nothing in comparison to making your first face-to-face call as the managing director, chief executive, chairman, or supreme allied commander of your own business.

APEX – The Ultimate Acronym

Whether preparing to make your first call, or your hundredth, there are some basic considerations. Although I am as sceptical as the next person of snappy acronyms, you could sum up your plans as APEX – Appearance, Preparation, Enthusiasm, and eXpertise.

APPEARANCE

A whole industry has been spawned by the importance of appearance. Imported from the US – where it seems that every businessman wears a dark blue suit with trousers that are a little bit too short, a woven silk tie with diagonal stripes, white cotton Oxford shirt and black brogues – the style consultants try to help us on how to look more powerful and confident. Although the idea may be distasteful, the concept is important: we need to project the right image, especially if there is nothing else to fall back on but ourselves. I agonized for ages over what I should wear to business meetings, before coming to the conclusion that I should look like one of the tribe. Basically, your appearance immediately marks you out: if you wear outrageous clothes, that is how your potential customer will see you. If you have avalanches of dandruff on your shoulders, it will also send a very strong message. You have to look like one of them – them being your customers. They want to empathize with.their suppliers; they don't want to be intimidated by them.

A small anecdote illustrates the point: during the 80s I did a lot of work in Eastern Europe, well before glasnost and peres-troika. I would call on clients who had little money for expensive clothes, and would kill for the chance to spend some time in Marks & Spencer. Some of my colleagues were from the US, and they used to dress pretty much as I've described above. The bill for one of their outfits probably ran to more than their average customer earnt in a month. But by far the most successful businessman I met on my travels was an American who worked for a huge computer company. He was indistinguishable from his clients: his hair was unfashionably long, he had specks of dandruff, he smoked, he wore brown polyester suits and man-made shoes. His customers loved him. I have no idea if he would go home in the evening and slip into a pair of Brooks Brothers trousers and a polo shirt, but that doesn't matter. He was completely in harmony with his audience, from the moment he came through their door.

The message is: don't be too eager to throw off the uniform from your life as an employee. That uniform, however drab it may appear to you, has a special significance. Change your appearance and you change people's perception of you. You must dress and look like the people with whom you're trying to do business.

PREPARATION

There is little point in pretending to be confident about making a sales call. Most of us dread them. There are so many things that can go wrong before, during and after a sales call that you might wonder whether there is anything positive about them. But solid preparation can limit the damage you can do to yourself.

Firstly, you have to know about the person and business you are going to visit. This sounds remarkably self-evident, but only the best salespeople actually bother to do the research. Consider builders who scan the pages of the local newspapers to see who is applying for planning permission: they know that this is a good way of introducing themselves, even though it may be laborious to get the information and follow up on it. Research is very tedious, but it pays dividends. Your prospective clients like to think that you have an interest in their business and, if you can prove that you know something about them, you will make a good impression. So find out as much as you can in advance of any meeting: read the local papers, go to the library, ask other people who may have some useful information.

Secondly, preparation extends to your own situation. You have to be prepared for the unexpected question, and the possibility that your prospect will want more information on what you can provide. Set yourself mentally so that you are expecting the unexpected. The thing you least expect on a first sales call – an agreement to do business – is the very thing that you must plan for. If you can respond immediately, the impression you create will be one of efficiency and confidence.

ENTHUSIASM

You've got the best product in the world. No one delivers the service like you do. However many times you say this to yourself in front of the mirror, it is very different when you're in front of a real live punter. Some years ago, a US research company undertook some very revealing analyses of why buyers believe that their suppliers are the best there is. They asked a group of companies to rank their bankers for a range of products and services. The researchers then asked the respondents why they had ranked the top banks as they had. In answer to the question, 'Why do you think this bank is the best?', over 80 per cent of respondents said, 'Because they told me they were'. Although this response is necessarily simplistic, it sends a very clear message to suppliers. If you are absolutely convinced of the quality of your product and service, the best way of convincing clients is to tell them of your conviction. Obviously, this is contingent upon a number of other factors – such as price – but the fact remains that customers like to be told that they are dealing with the best in the market.

The point is, you must not be defensive about what you're selling. When you're faced with the inevitable question – 'Why should I buy from you?' – it is all too easy to reply negatively: 'I'm cheaper than your current supplier' or 'You should always have an alternative'. These are defensive replies that say nothing about you and your unique selling points. You must exude enthusiasm and confidence; knocking the competition is hardly a very professional way of selling yourself. In answer to that question, you need to be able to put your hand on your heart and say: 'Because I'm the best'. You must, of course, be able to qualify that with some pretty solid reasons for this contention, but it is music to the ears of your prospective clients if they hear lots of positive signals about why they should use you.

EXPERTISE

No one is expecting you to be a sales natural. Selling is a skill that can be taught and learnt, and there are good (and bad) teachers and sales courses, if you feel inclined to use them. But remember that buying is a skill as well, and you can be trained in that, too. Don't expect that your prospect will have no experience of buying, or of making life extremely difficult for you. A seasoned buyer can identify sales techniques very easily, and knows how to evade them.

In your first days of business, however, you're not going to have enough time and money to go on training courses and, quite frankly, you don't need to. What you do need is confidence, and you can get this for free. Your product, you believe, is the best. You've drawn up a list of features and benefits, and these are obviously compelling. You've researched your target clients, so you know what their needs are likely to be. When you step into their office, you are there as the person best qualified to represent yourself and whatever it is you are supplying. The prospect is there to be convinced: they've given you some of their valuable time to listen to your case, and you owe it to yourself, and them, to present it as effectively as you can.

So remember that you are the expert. You have expertise in the market, in your product and service, and in understanding client requirements. All this must come across during the sales call. Buyers know when someone is bluffing, and they give them very short shrift. You must be armed with facts, confidently delivered. Once you are in a position where you have established your credibility as a potential supplier, everything else will fall into place much more naturally, and the way to achieve this is by looking and sounding completely confident and assured about the market, the customer, and your ability to fulfil their requirements. You'll only get one opportunity to do this, so don't waste it.

The Faithful Servants

APEX is all about planning for that sales call. What is more difficult is managing the actual call. How do you sell or, better still, make the punter buy? However much research and preparation you've done, there's still great scope for things to go very differently once you're in front of the prospect. So the call is not just about presenting your own product – it's also about discovery. You want to discover as much as possible about the buyer, about their wishes and aspirations, and there are six easy ways to do this. 'The six faithful servants', as Kipling described them, are: who, what, why, when, where and how. Every question you ask – bar one, which we'll come on to later – should begin with one of these. Who in your company is going to make a decision about this? What are the most important buying criteria for you? Why do you like the service you're getting now? When will you be making a decision? Where would I have to supply my service? How is a decision made? These are the types of question that you should be asking. They are all open-ended, meaning that it's impossible to answer 'yes' or 'no' to them. They all elicit further information, which you can then use to your advantage.

The typical structure of a sales call goes something like this: the supplier introduces the concept of what is on offer, and then asks these open-ended questions to get the prospect to open up and give some indication of what is important. The supplier then translates that information and presents a list of reasons why the service matches the criteria of the buyer. The supplier – you – has to make the product match the buyer's requirements, not the other way round. If you cannot do that, you're not going to get an order. Although this sounds ludicrously simple, it doesn't often work that way. Too many sales people simply pull rabbits out of the hat, hoping that something they say will ring a bell. They don't spend enough time asking the critical questions that will tell them what it is that the buyer needs. Selling is all about listening. If you don't listen to, and understand, what the buyer is saying, you'll stand very little chance of making a sale.

Getting to 'No'

You also face the possibility that, no matter what you say and how confidently you say it, the buyer simply isn't interested. This is frustrating, but it happens more often than you'd think, and there are any number of reasons for it. Perhaps they misunderstood you on the phone; perhaps they are using you simply as a bargaining weapon against their current suppliers; or, most frighteningly, perhaps you haven't done your homework properly and you've missed the target. Whatever the reason, you must withdraw gracefully and learn from the experience. Every interaction with a potential client teaches you something, if you're prepared to learn. Don't brood on failures; simply move on to the next prospect and do a better job next time.

Ask for the Business

I mentioned that there is one question which should not be prefaced by one of those six faithful servants. That question is: 'Can I have your business?' Of course, you don't need to put it quite like that, but the thrust of the question must be the same, and it must demand a 'Yes' or 'No' answer. You need to know when to ask it, but this will eventually become instinctive. If you've asked the right questions, and turned the answers into powerful arguments for buying what you're selling, you'll stand a good chance of making a sale. The vast majority of sales people, skilled or not, never ask for the business. They simply assume that, having made their case, the buyer is going to volunteer to become a customer. But it doesn't work like that. Asking for someone's business is one of the most powerful things you can do: it puts the buyer on the spot, and demonstrates how keen you are. The disappointing fact is that you may be fobbed off with responses like: 'I'll think about it', or 'I have to speak to some colleagues', but you've set the ball rolling, committing the prospect to action. Occasionally, they might simply say 'Yes': I can assure you that this is the best feeling there is, and very much more than compensates for all the hard grind that prefaced it.

Following Up

Follow-up is one of the great chores. You get back to your base, throw off the uniform and sit at your desk, elated and relieved at having completed the call. Now you need to do some analysis. You need to work out what went well, and what could have gone better. If the buyer asked for more information, you'll need to put it together. Sometimes you'll be asked for a proposal, or a quote. Don't be fooled by this – a buyer can put you off the scent by asking you to bid on something, because they know you'll be very eager to do it and it puts all the onus back on you. A proposal should never be issued until you're 90 per cent sure that you're going to get the business; in effect, it should be an affirmation of terms and conditions already agreed during face-to-face meetings and phone calls. It should not be a sales tool. Many major organizations measure the success of their sales force by the number of proposals that are sent out, and the sales force can then avoid responsibility for failure by blaming lost business on the product or the pricing. The best sales manager I ever worked for didn't care about proposal or quote generation: he wanted to see his sales team making calls, seeing people, spreading the word. One successful proposal is worth immeasurably more than one hundred failures, and yet we all get sucked into believing that the preparation of a quote is a sign of success. So be very careful about responding to these requests, especially when you don't feel you have enough information to make a rational proposal.

Whatever you've been asked to do, make sure you react quickly and comprehensively. If you have heated up a prospect, you need to keep them hot. If they have to wait 10 days to hear from you, they'll go off the boil. Remember the first priority of any business – whether it's run from the attic of 32 Acacia Avenue or the City of London – is the acquisition of new customers. At the beginning of your life as a micro-entrepreneur, nothing else matters. Sometimes you'll feel as if you are wasting your time, especially when prospects don't react to your approaches. But you can never rule out a prospect simply because they don't sign up at the first time of asking. You never know when their priorities will change, and you need to have created a good impression so that they immediately think of you if they're considering changing suppliers.

KISS – Keep It Simple, Stupid

Another significant danger for the sole trader is to slip into the language of big business. If you've been used to working for a big employer, it's very hard to get out of the habit of writing and saying things that mean absolutely nothing. Make your proposals, and all your correspondence, as brief as you can, in plain English. Thank the prospect for giving you the opportunity to discuss their business, and summarize the key points of your discussion. Emphasize the unique selling points of your own service, and make those relevant to the prospect's situation. Don't waffle – keep on editing your correspondence until it is as short as you can possibly make it.

Once you've done this, you must follow up with a phone call. Give the prospect time to read your letter – 7 to 10 days is probably about the right length of time – and then call to see what they think of it. This call will be a vital part of the selling process, showing that you're interested in pursuing the business and available to answer any further questions. Offer them the opportunity of another meeting, but don't do this if it will just prolong the process. You'll soon learn how to distinguish between someone who is really interested, and someone who is stringing you along.

Thanks, but No Thanks

Earlier in the book I mentioned the advice of a consultant, who told me to judge each opportunity on its merits. Every so often, a prospect will approach you with an idea that falls well outside your normal line of business, and it presents you with a dilemma. You're being offered the opportunity to bid on a piece of business that might bring in a lot of money, but that will require you to do things that weren't in your original plan. Before making a decision on whether to proceed you need to analyse a number of issues.

Firstly, ask yourself some simple questions. What do you really want to do? Are you happy with the way the business is going (remembering that happiness is the most important part of being a sole trader)? Is the revenue sufficient? Will it sustain you long-term? If the answer to any of these is no, then you have a reason for considering other lines of business. But you also have to worry about why the prospect is asking you to do something different. Is it because no one else will do it – the Assignment from Hell? Is it because they like you and want to give you more business, even though they know it falls outside your normal remit? Or are they simply ignorant of what you can and can't do?

Turning down business is the one thing that no sole trader wants to do. You've made such an effort to get to the point where punters are approaching you, and there you are saying 'No'. It hurts – but it can be the only sensible alternative. If the opportunity looks like being a major problem, and you doubt your ability to fulfil it professionally, you should definitely refuse. However, there are ways to turn down business without causing undue offence.

A bald refusal is not a good idea. A prospective customer has made the effort to get in touch, thinking justifiably that you will be very pleased to be offered some business. The very least you can do is demonstrate your appreciation for that offer, even if you have no intention of taking it up. Bear in mind that customers are looking for solutions, however straightforward or complex their problem may be, and that is what suppliers provide. A solution doesn't necessarily involve you having to do the work that's on offer. Later on in the book we'll look at alternative methods of fulfilling customer needs, but the basic principle is that you must always act as a facilitator in this process. You want to be perceived by customers, whether live or potential, as being helpful and accommodating.

An Opportunity, Not a Problem

The best sales people understand this, and will never say: 'We can't (or don't, or won't) do that.' Instead, when faced with a request that is outside their normal line of work, they will answer the question with another question: 'Why do you need that?'. By asking this, you are eliciting more information on the customer's motivations, which is the key to successful selling. Perhaps the buyer has heard of some new way of doing business, or a twist on service or product features, from a competitor, and has decided that this is now a very important element in the buying process. But, as often as not, what they have been offered does not intrinsically enhance the value of the product: it's merely a gimmick, a feature without a benefit. An example might be a 24-hour hotline for customer enquiries, useful if you're buying emergency plumbing services but of questionable value if you're using a management consultant or an interior decorator. Why is that perceived as being important to the client? Once you know the answer, you can decide whether you have to match it, or whether you can reasonably refuse or offer a more useful alternative.

If, however, the offer is more difficult to deal with, you have to look at different ways of dealing with it. Say you're a headhunter – sorry, an executive-search consultant – specializing in financial services, and a client asks you to conduct a search in the fast-moving consumer-goods sector. There's a lot of income at stake, but you have no experience in that particular field. You could turn it down, but that blocks your ability to earn more money and, more importantly, it effectively gives the buyer the impression that, forever more, you are not interested in this line of work. This is where your network is so important. As a headhunter, you will undoubtedly know other headhunters, and they may well be interested in the assignment and have the expertise that you lack. Much as it may upset you to offer work to one of your competitors, you can comfort yourself with two thoughts: firstly, you are offering a solution to the customer and, if you structure the deal correctly, you can earn some commission from your competitor for doing very little work. The mechanics of this will be looked at in more detail later on, but you have to keep an open mind on how you earn your living. As long as the customer is satisfied, and you can sleep at night, these types of deals are worth considering.

Learning the Three Cs

Is there such a thing as a natural salesperson? I don't think there is. In fact, we all start life as great salespeople. Children have an uncanny knack of knowing exactly how to get what they want out of their parents. Mum says that little Johnny can only have one sweet; Johnny asks for three, with the most adorable look on his face; Mum says two maximum, and Johnny has negotiated a 100 per cent increase of the original deal! The sole trader has to use skills that are slightly better developed than this, but the principles are the same.

Selling successfully is all about the three Cs: confidence, competence and communication. Confidence comes from knowing about your prospective customers, their needs, their criteria for buying; competence is all about knowing your own strengths and weaknesses, focusing on the former whilst working hard to eradicate the latter; and communication is concerned with getting the message across to your chosen audience, in a way that reinforces the aura of success that you want to surround your business. Understanding and implementing this is absolutely critical if you are going to make it in the world of the sole trader. Selling is a lonely skill, especially when you're working for yourself. It exposes you in a way that no other experience can but, when it goes well, there's no greater thrill you can have with your clothes on.

Sadly, that's not even the half of it. Successful selling drives businesses forward; but successful relationship management, where you keep customers happy, is what really pays the bills. For the self-employed, retaining customers is the most difficult part of all. A customer who uses you once is useful; a customer who keeps on paying you is worth their weight in gold.

Chapter Six

STAYING FRIENDS

The greatest excitement in your life as a sole trader is when someone says 'Yes', that glorious moment when prospect is transformed into customer. When this happens for the first time – and when you realize that you have successfully led them to a decision to buy – you run through a remarkably comprehensive series of emotions. You'll be elated, naturally, whatever the value of the bargain; you'll panic, as you realize that you've got to deliver the goods; you'll worry, wondering how you're going to do it again; and you'll dream, thinking of how you are going to spend the money that will soon be yours.

Additionally, first sales can lead to severe depression. You soon learn, after the initial euphoria, that a single sale is not going to sustain you in the manner to which you'd like to become accustomed, and you are going to have to repeat the process many times. You also wonder whether you priced your service properly: it's very rare to complete a sale without worrying about the pricing, and success can lead to concern about how profitable the business is going to be. And you now have a demanding client to deal with, on top of all the other complications of running your own business. Your whole focus must change: suddenly you have more than one priority, as customers and prospects vie for your attention. You feel as if you will never have enough time to deal with the often conflicting requirements of these two constituencies, let alone handle all the administration.

Keep Them Coming

In the next chapter we'll deal with planning for all this work but, for now, we need to focus on your customers. Above all, you want to make sure that you become the preferred supplier to all your existing clients, and there are many ways to do this. Existing clients will be the easiest source of new business: as mentioned earlier, research suggests that it costs five times more to win business from a new client as it does to gain more from an existing one. Whatever you are selling, whatever the frequency of purchase, your customers must be taught to think of you first. Customer loyalty is hard to achieve, and easy to lose. Another statistic demonstrates the point: as an average, customers who are satisfied with their suppliers tend to tell 5 other people about it, whilst those who are dissatisfied are likely to tell 25 others about their annoyance. But, once you've got your customers hooked, the benefits are enormous: they come to you, beating a path to your door and cutting out much of the sales effort that takes up so much of your time.

Why do customers stay with a supplier? The answer is very simple: service. Service is not easy to define, but encompasses all the peripheral aspects of the product that differentiate it from its competition. It may include price, but that will rarely be the sole factor. More often, service is all about delivering what you promised to deliver. One of the better nostrums of the salesman is to 'underpromise and overdeliver'. You manage customer expectations by promising only what is definitely achievable: if you match or exceed those promises, your customer is likely to be happy.

Buyers are a conservative breed. Once they have found a product that they can trust, they are naturally inclined to use it over and over again. This conservatism extends from toothpaste to the most complex computer systems. But, whilst this conservatism works in your favour once you have customers, it also means that you have to work very hard to prove to them that they should switch to you from another supplier. Once you have proved that, you need to reiterate it with superior service.

The Ultimate Goal: Customer Delight

Unfortunately, you are unlikely to have learnt very much about customer service with your ex-employer. Good customer service is something of an oxymoron in the UK; in many businesses, customers are considered to be a monumental pain in the neck. They're demanding, ungrateful time-wasters. And you will almost undoubtedly have been on the receiving end of this attitude at some stage, whether in a restaurant or a banking hall. The major business successes of the last decade have been those – like Virgin, Direct Line Insurance, Dell Computers and Sainsbury's – that have spent time analysing what customers are looking for, and have set out to deliver it. Nothing revolutionary in this, you might think, but the demand for customer delight is growing.

And delight is the word that should always be uppermost in your mind. Satisfaction is not really enough: customers should be delighted with your service. In Japan, some companies actually have customer delight managers! Model yourself on that, and aim for delight: don't be satisfied with satisfaction.

Setting the Tone

So how do you actually go about delighting customers, consistently matching or exceeding their requirements and expectations? Although there are no templates for success, and each customer will want something a little bit different, there are some basic principles that apply to every product, and to every buyer. The process of customer service actually begins well before a sale is made: the impression you make during the sales cycle will establish much of the foundation for the relationship with your customers once you've sold something to them. Go back to that acronym, APEX – appearance, preparation, enthusiasm and expertise – and think about how each one of those factors will influence the buyer's perception of you. That perception will stick in the buyer's mind as the embodiment of how you will deliver your product, how you will serve them once you have a contract. That perception must match up with reality: where it doesn't, you will always be managing a big gap between what your customers want and what you supply. The bad news is that this gap will always be there, and your task is to keep it as small as possible. Customers nearly always expect more than they receive, but this is actually no bad thing: it makes suppliers strive harder to improve their products and services in an effort to close the gap.

Service Blueprinting

If your sales and marketing activity delineates initial customer impressions, then it makes sense to have a very clear picture in your mind of how you will position yourself so that the service you provide is consistent with those impressions. One of the more recent fashions in management philosophy is the idea of service blueprinting. As a concept, it is relatively straightforward, and can be applied equally well to sole traders as to multinational conglomerates.

With service blueprinting, you draw a diagram of the product delivery process, incorporating everything you need to do to fulfil a customer order. In most cases you can split the diagram into two: activities that are above the line, i.e. those that will be seen by the customer, and activities that are below the line, and will remain unseen. Once you have drawn this blueprint, you can identify those tasks that are most likely to cause concern to your customer should they not be performed as promised – fail-points – and, just as importantly, you can look at areas which, whilst appearing to be below the customers' line of visibility, will also upset them if they go wrong.

Fail-points most commonly occur where you rely on someone else to provide a part of the service. If you're an interior designer, for example, and you make a commitment to have a project completed by a certain date, you set up inherent fail-points if your supplier doesn't send you the chintz curtain material when you need it, or your friendly curtain-maker falls ill. Dealing with these fail-points means that you have to have contingency plans – more than one curtain-maker, for instance – to cover all eventualities. As a sole trader, you are probably the single biggest fail-point, especially if you are selling something that is based entirely on your own abilities.

Blueprinting is also useful because it highlights areas that you might not otherwise have concerned yourself about. A major high-street bank will send out millions of highly confidential letters, statements and advices during the course of the year, and it will spend a lot of time and money over the design of these. But who in the bank worries about the media through which all this correspondence is delivered? If the central purchasing department buys envelopes that routinely pop open because the gum is low quality, the whole effort is ruined. This purchasing activity is definitely below the line of customer visibility, and yet potentially it will have an enormous impact on the customers' perception of that bank's service.

Bringing it down to the level of the sole trader, you need to worry about these small things that assume such huge importance in your customers' minds. If your contact is called Smyth, and you consistently spell his name Smith, that will annoy him. If he changes his address or phone number, and has the courtesy to tell you about it, then you should make sure you change your database. These sound like silly examples, but they're not: you really have no idea what will alter the customer's perception of your service, so you have to cover every eventuality and present the most professional face that you possibly can.

Blueprinting doesn't need to take up much of your time, but you must do it to some extent, even if only on the back of an envelope (a good quality one, of course!). If you are forearmed with the knowledge of how your service can go wrong, you'll be much better placed to avoid it happening.

Staying on Track

Once you have mapped out your service capabilities, you have to move from theory to practice. You have to remember what your prospect told you during the sales process: what were the top priorities? The danger for any business, of whatever size, is that the sales process is completely divorced from the rest of the process. Sales people make calls, write call reports, win deals, bring back contracts, and then move on to the next prospect. They may have negotiated special deals, unusual service levels, changes to pricing, or a thousand other wrinkles to the standard product offering and, as likely as not, the people charged with fulfilling all these arrangements have not been consulted. As a sole trader, this won't happen to you – after all, you're head of sales, client relations, operations, finance and administration – but you may well have promised things to your client that, in the cold light of day after a deal is struck, seem rather onerous and difficult to achieve.

This problem is multiplied by the number of customers you have. Very few of us can afford to take our product to the market and say: 'Here it is. Take it or leave it.' We all have to make compromises; it is one of the reasons why small businesses are successful, because they are flexible enough to adapt to customer requirements. All your instincts should tell you that, within reason, you will need to follow where your customer leads. He has the money, and you want it.

But you have to make a judgement as to how far you are prepared to stray from your original plan to ensure you get the business. Making sales can become so addictive that you begin to believe that a sale at any cost is worth the pain it will subsequently bring. This is especially true if your bank balance looks particularly unhealthy, or there is a lull in the market. All sole traders have made sales that we have come to regret, either because the pricing was low or the work we were asked to do did not fit in with our overall strategy. You shouldn't worry about this too much, but it shouldn't become a habit either. And it's worth considering some of the evidence of the case studies, which shows how customers can convince you that there is a different product you could be offering that will give you much more scope for success.

No News is not Good News

The critical issue in maintaining a good relationship with your customers is communication. Customers like to know what's going on. You already know this from your role as a customer: you sit in a restaurant and wait 45 minutes for your main course to arrive. Supercilious waiters breeze past with orders for other diners, ignoring you as you try to catch their eye. But, if they came up to you and politely explained the situation and reasons for the delay, offering you a complimentary glass of wine, you'd feel pacified. In exactly the same way, your buyers do not want to be kept in the dark. They do not want to have to ring you to find out the fate of their order; they want you to communicate with them, updating them on your progress. Communication is part of the product, part of the service.

There's a tendency to believe that communication should only take place if there's a problem: if you are doing your job, and everything's going well, it's all too easy to believe that nothing needs to be said to the customer. But that's patently inaccurate: you have no idea of what your customer is thinking. They may be sitting in their office fretting about their decision to use you, and a thundering silence will merely reinforce their doubts. The use of a judicious phone call can allay all these fears. You ring to update them on the progress of the order, reassuring them and demonstrating your professionalism and commitment. It takes five minutes, and the customer goes away with a nice warm feeling. It also gives you the opportunity to talk generally: never underestimate the power of a friendly chat that seems to have no particular agenda. The customer, at ease and comforted by your call, may volunteer some useful information that you can use when you want to sell to him again.

Problem Management

Problems are more difficult to handle. Remember that every interaction you have with a customer, whether face to face, by letter or on the phone, is a test of your selling skills. If you have to break bad news – the curtain material hasn't arrived, your dog is sick, you're in the middle of a tax audit – you have to wrap it up effectively so that there is a problem and a solution. Again, learn from your own experience: when someone disappoints you, you want them to offer you a reason and a good alternative to what was on offer. You've had your heart set on a new car in an especially jazzy colour, and the dealer takes your order, only to ring back later and say that the colour you wanted isn't available for six months. What does the dealer say to you that will make you less disappointed? He offers you a little discount if you take a different colour, or comes up with an alternative that sustains your excitement about getting the car.

In exactly the same way, you must plan the way in which you deliver bad news. Remember that your customers want you to succeed; they have a vested interest in seeing you thrive and prosper, not only because they may have some latent longing to do exactly what you're doing, and strike out on their own, but also because they chose you in the first place and they don't wish to be made to look foolish. So honesty is really the best policy, painful as it may be to follow it. Explain the problem, propose a solution – and don't forget to apologize.

Research and Development

If the objective is to build a loyal core of delighted customers, you'll have to devote a lot of attention to them. Customers like to be stroked; they like to be made to feel important, valuable human beings whose opinions are actively sought and considered. This is the fundamental principle that drives your product development process. You cannot hope to improve your product and service unless you have the input of customers to use as guidance. In large firms, armies of product-development managers pore over research and analyse competitive offerings to come up with a better mousetrap. In exactly the same way, albeit on a lesser scale, you will have to do your own research to discover what the market wants and where its requirements are heading.

Your product cannot stand still; you cannot remain insulated from developments elsewhere and hope that your buyers will ignore them. So you have to establish a routine that allows you to gather data on what your customers think of you and your offering, and what non-customers would need to convince them to buy from you. Look at the case study of the management consultant, Edward: he estimates that 50 per cent of his time is spent on business promotion. This is not simply made up of lots of calls on suspects/prospects, but is also concerned with polling opinions from all sectors of the market he serves.

There are several ways to gather this information. Naturally, you want to maintain continuous dialogue with clients, regardless of whether you are in the middle of a transaction with them. Customers are normally flattered to be asked for their opinion, a fact you already know from your own experience as a buyer. You feel good if you are asked what you think of a particular service, and if it seems as if the request is being made with a serious intention to improve that service as a result of the response you give. But talking to customers is by no means the only way of taking the temperature of your market.

Surveys can provide you with an excellent snapshot of your customers' perception of you and your product. Written surveys are used widely in business: where they tend to score over verbal communication is that they are more widely circulated within the buyer's office, getting the opinion of people with whom you might not normally have any contact. If you are selling to one person, but your service is being used by others, a written survey can draw out all the differing perceptions within the buying organization. But a survey is worthless if the results are not acted upon: so often, they are used as a smokescreen by companies who want to look as if they are interested in their customers' views, but who really have little incentive or motivation to change. If you decide to send out a survey, you must be prepared to do the follow-up work; you must accept that what respondents say may not be to your liking, and that you will have to change as a result.

No one medium of communication can ensure that you have the total picture: that's one of the frustrating things about relationship management. So keeping close to the market – reading trade journals, talking to others who operate in the same area – is a continuous function. Every opinion you gather is like a photograph, or the result of a general election: it may record the sentiment at that particular moment, but it will have little validity in three or six months' time.

Courting Clients

Are customers corruptible? 'Every man has his price', so they say. Don't worry – I'm not suggesting that you leave plain brown envelopes stuffed with crisp fivers taped behind the cistern in the customer's lavatory. But buyers, in spite of occasional indications to the contrary, are only human. We all know that the business of corporate hospitality is now a multi-million pound industry, with no major or minor sporting event complete without the rows of hospitality tents and marquees. Perhaps Centre Court seats for the men's final at Wimbledon will stretch your budget a little too far, but the concept of hospitality is one that should be in the forefront of your mind. Taking a customer and their spouse to dinner, or to the theatre, is a very powerful weapon in your armoury, as it achieves a number of objectives. It shows you care about them, and want to demonstrate your appreciation for their business; it takes you both out of the work environment and into a more relaxed atmosphere, allowing you to size each other up socially; and it enables you to say a little bit about yourself – both by the entertainment you choose and the way in which you behave – that might otherwise remain unsaid.

Don't be fooled, however, into believing that you will win lots of additional business on the strength of a good dinner or two tickets for an Eric Clapton concert. Buyers are hard-headed enough to put that to one side when they are considering a purchase. But entertaining them, and putting them at their ease in a social setting, allows you to understand them much better – and vice versa. Corporate hospitality is a means of saying thank you, but is also a more subtle way of learning how your customers think, what their motivations are, and what interests them. You never know when this knowledge may come in useful. It's not unheard of for customers to entertain you, either: they may have exactly the same reasons as you do, but you should always accept an invitation from a customer. Who knows where it might lead?

When you sign up as a member of the sole-trader community, you sign up to a life that will be driven by your customers. This is a major shift in the balance of power for many of us who were formerly employees: in that life, we believed that we answered to our boss. Very few us had direct, daily contact with the customers who ultimately paid our salaries. Have you ever seen an organization chart that had customers at the top of it, to whom everyone ultimately reported? Of course not – because large companies just don't make enough effort to imbue their staff with the realization that the customer is king (or queen). But you, as the sole trader, are only answerable to them: everything you do must be motivated by what your customers require, what they consider to be important. This is such a major sea-change for many of us that it can be frightening in the extreme. One of the main reasons for going it alone is to escape from the slavery of working for someone else, to put yourself firmly in control of your own destiny. But, ultimately, everyone is answerable to someone else: directors are harried by shareholders, writers have to satisfy their publishers and readers, gurus have to keep their disciples happy. As a sole trader, at least you have a very clear idea of who is paying you, and to whom you are answerable. If you cannot accept the primacy of the customer, you should not embark upon the life of a micro-entrepreneur. But if you can, then you'll be repaid – and you might even have some fun in the meantime.

Chapter Seven

MINDING YOUR Ps

Very conveniently, many of the issues that you face as a sole trader start with the letter P – product, pricing, promotion, provision, planning, problems, pipeline, partnerships, and potential. In earlier chapters we've looked at the first four – how to position your product, pricing implications, sales and marketing and the delivery of your service – and now we must deal with the grab-bag of 'Ps' that are left.

PLANNING

Planning for the sole trader is almost a contradiction in terms. Especially in the early days, everything is so immediate, and so important, that the future is dimly perceived and often entirely overlooked. But to plan effectively is vital if you are to follow your chosen path: an absence of planning will result in you becoming stale, unenthusiastic, morose and depressed. When that happens, your motivation disappears, and your thoughts return to the idea of 'safe' employment – definitely not a good idea.

The Eternal Concern

What do you need to plan for? Essentially, there' are two major issues to be considered, inseparable and equally important. Firstly, you will always be worrying about money; of all the people interviewed for the case studies, not one suggested that finance had become less of an issue as their businesses progressed.

For most sole traders, there will be periods of feast and famine, dictated by cash flow and work-in-progress. It is most unlikely that the majority of us will ever reach that virtuous position where money simply isn't an issue – and, if you have done, you should skip this section now and go back to your yacht.

At the beginning of your life as a sole trader, you worked out your known expenditures, and how they would be covered and exceeded by the income you hoped to generate. Occasionally this will need updating as your circumstances change, but that isn't really planning, that's just tinkering. To plan effectively, you need to have an objective: clearly, the primary aim when you start off is to keep the wolf from the door, but you'll need to look much further ahead than this. How will you fund your pension? What will you be doing in 10, 15, 20 years' time? Are you always going to be self-employed, or are you using this period to enhance your employability – and, if so, when do you hope to move back into that market? What do you want for your family and dependents? These questions so easily get lost in the maze of all the other considerations you're dealing with every day, and you must give yourself the time to think about them, and come up with some realistic answers. You cannot expect yourself to plan about the future in those idle moments when you're sitting at your desk with nothing to do – you must carve out some quality time to give serious thought to your circumstances, and how you want them to be changed by your own endeavours.

Like everything else that is a prediction, planning is an imprecise science. That doesn't make it any less valid or valuable, because the plan can change as often as your objectives do. But it's good to have a map of your future, one that will make the work you are doing now seem much more relevant in the light of what you hope to achieve. Most of us would be horrified if we thought that we would be doing the same thing in 10 years' time as we are now but, unlike employees whose employers help them to shape their career and provide them with new challenges, sole traders have only one person to rely on for the direction of their

life. You have to make the right moves, some of which will come
through serendipity, but most of which will only happen if you
plan to make them happen.

Expecting the Unexpected

Planning starts on day one of your new life as a micro-entrepreneur. Whatever your idea is for a business, and however clever it
may be, it is unlikely to sustain you for the rest of your working
life. In many businesses, technology will progressively replace
people, for instance: can you predict when and if this will happen
to you, and what your reaction will be? Planning is anticipating
the expected and the unexpected – things that you're pretty sure
will occur and things about which you can be much less certain.
Either way, you don't want to end up being overtaken by events:
you must always have a Plan B.

If money is one reason for planning, the other is peace of
mind. Go back to your days as an employee: however grudgingly,
you have to accept that there are benefits to having someone else
take care of many aspects of your life, such as regular pay, a
pension plan, National Insurance and PAYE, and any other
benefits on offer. These aspects of your life, all of which will now
be totally under your control, can assume unreasonable status in
your mind if you haven't had the foresight to plan for them, and
how they will continue to be serviced for the rest of your working
days. Additionally, you want the reassurance and comfort of
knowing that you can, by choice, continue to work for yourself
for as long as it pleases you. Having this knowledge then puts
you in a position where you can more easily consider all the
opportunities and alternatives that are presented to you.

Why Bother?

If this all sounds fanciful and somewhat utopian, I can sympathize with you. Committing yourself to the life of a sole trader is highly stimulating, and you carry a lot of instinctive, and completely necessary, optimism with you. This optimism, whilst wholly laudable, is one of the very reasons why planning seems to be so unnecessary: why plan, you say to yourself, when I know that everything's going to work out just as I'd hoped and I'm going to make lots of money? Yes, but . . . the world doesn't see things in quite the same light. Specifically, your chosen client base may have a completely different perspective on your ideas and how they want to use you, if at all. And you should bear in mind that your competitors won't be standing idly by, watching you as you gallop off with all their customers.

Regardless of whether you hit upon the Big Idea or not, you're going to face the problem of how long you can sustain your business in its existing format. Planning for the future is critical in maintaining your momentum and motivation. Inevitably, however, few of us are able to plan too far ahead: we become so engrossed in the immediate problems and opportunities confronting us every day that we tend to lose sight of the longer term aspects of our lives as independent operators.

The message is this: by all means be optimistic, and set yourself ambitious personal and professional targets. But don't expect that they will be achieved unless you've put in the necessary groundwork to position yourself for success, and to protect yourself from disaster when things don't go according to plan.

PROBLEMS

Whichever fathead said that a problem is really an opportunity in disguise should be shot. When you're wondering how to pay the tax man, and that cheque that your customer promised had been sent hasn't arrived, it's difficult to see how you can turn this into an opportunity. The plans that you make for financing, business expansion, personal satisfaction and all those other wonderful dreams can crumble to nothing if you haven't got the initiative and determination to deal with problems.

Sole traders often feel that they're completely alone, that it's up to them to make things happen and deal with the crises single-handedly. To a certain extent, that's true: you no longer have a boss to take your worries to, and you learn to act independently. But most problems look much bigger to you than to anyone else and, the more you allow them to fester, the greater the import-ance they assume. 'A problem shared is a problem halved', so the saying goes and, although I hate these old saws as much as you probably do, there's an element of truth to this one. There is a whole army of problem-solvers out there waiting to hear from you. Some will charge you for the privilege, but many won't.

Ask for Help

What kind of problems are you likely to encounter? They fall into a number of categories – financial, administrative, personal, product, supply – but there are normally solutions waiting for them (especially if you've done your planning properly). Financial problems lie at the heart of most sole traders' worries: money doesn't come in when you thought it would, your expenditure is higher than you anticipated, a customer defaults on payment. This is where some prudent planning, and the use of professional help, can reap dividends. We've already considered the indispens-ability of a good accountant – I've lost count of the money and anguish mine has saved me over the years. Accountants aren't just there to add up the pluses and minuses of your business, they're there to give advice and dig you out of holes. They're also much better qualified to negotiate with creditors, get tough with debtors and put in a good word with your bank manager. Choose your accountant with care: find one that understands the dynamics of the small business, and get a deal so that you pay them a retainer for ongoing advice and counsel. Accountants' fees may look high, but they're a good investment if things go wrong, so you should treat them as an insurance policy.

Reserves of Strength

An accountant cannot conjure up money from nowhere, however, so you must create a reserve. You obviously hope to live within your means, but there will be times when, however good the long-term prospects are, you will have to dip into separate funds to keep you going. I maintain that this fund should be created out of the income you earn, rather than any redundancy money you might have received; on a regular basis, you should move money from your business account to a savings account. It's unlikely that you'll be able to set up a standing order to do this, because your cash flow will be so unpredictable, but make an effort to move some money every month, however little it may be. You don't want to end up raiding little Johnny's piggy bank to pay your stationery bill.

If you can hold onto any credit facilities that you had as an employee, so much the better, but remember that banks take a very dim view of the self-employed and are likely to review, if not cancel, all those facilities once you have no regular income coming in. Many of the case studies claimed that they did not have a problem with their bank, mainly because they never went overdrawn. Here again, your accountant can be very helpful: they know the banks and the specific managers who are sympathetic to the requirements and tribulations of the sole trader, and they can put you in touch with a good introduction. There's nothing to say that you shouldn't separate your business and personal banking relationships between different financial institutions.

Reserving is tough. You get a cheque in the mail and it's difficult not to allocate all the money immediately. But it's all part of the planning process, and the best sole traders manage it.

The Cheque's in the Mail

More problematic is when you don't get a cheque in the mail. For me, the most exciting part of the working day is when the postman arrives: there's always the prospect of a cheque or two, and who knows what else – an invitation to tender for some new business, a thank you letter from an appreciative client, some news on an opportunity never heard of before? But the absence of income from debtors is likely to cause extreme discomfort. How do you approach the problem of late payers?

On your invoices you should always include the terms of payment. These may include a discount for prompt settlement, and a overall timeframe in which the invoice should be paid. Many large customers will routinely assume that they get 30 days' credit automatically: in fact, many only have a cheque run once a month. The sole trader has some interesting and unique problems here: you can have a fantastic relationship with your buyers, who have your best interests at heart and understand your need to collect money quickly but, if they don't communicate that to their accounts department, it counts for very little. One trader I know has invested a considerable amount of time in learning exactly who is responsible for paying the bills in each company he deals with. This is a smart move: being on friendly terms with the guys who write the cheques is a very powerful weapon. He knows that when his invoice hits their desk they will recognise it and give it a fair wind through the tortuous payment process. Try and do the same thing: find out from your contacts who will actually pay your bills, and make the effort to get to know them.

Another issue is size: as a sole trader, your individual invoices may be relatively small. Perversely, this can delay payment. The smaller the invoice, the less attention it is likely to receive. I had one customer who insisted that my invoices should be split into smaller amounts, because it helped his internal approval process. It helped him, but it didn't do much for my cash flow: these bills simply weren't given any priority. There's no easy solution to this.

Pay-as-you-go

If you're fortunate enough to be doing a lot of work for the same company, and you've proved yourself to be reliable and honest, you can get paid for work-in-progress. This is an accepted business practice: you bill for the work as you go along. You can ask for an up-front payment, to get you started at the beginning of a contract, and receive regular payments as the project advances. This is particularly useful for consultants who work on projects over a longer period, and for traders who incur substantial costs at the beginning of a job, such as for buying materials or hiring other outside help. Regularizing your income does wonders for your cash flow, and should be one of your main financial objectives.

But late payers will always exist, some wilfully, some by accident. Very few of us can afford to run credit checks on potential customers and they have a limited value in any case. Many of us make the mistake of believing that the bigger the client, the less risk there is of being paid late or not at all. Experience has made us wiser, especially if you have the misfortune to deal with any agency of government: for all their talk of the harmful effects of late payment to small businesses, they are often the worst offenders.

The Final Solution

If you have done your job properly, and are still waiting to be paid, you have a number of alternatives for recovering the money. You can try to sue, but that is absolutely the last resort. A solicitor's letter can cost a lot, and almost inevitably leads to bad feeling between you and your customer, with whom you may hope to do business again. Unpaid invoices happen for a number of reasons, so you need to find out exactly what the problem is before you wade in with the full force of the law behind you.

The single biggest reason, in my experience, is inefficiency. You send an invoice to your client, they approve and sign it, and then pop it in the internal mail to their accounts department. It never shows up at its intended destination. It probably doesn't happen quite as often as buyers would have you believe, but it is always worth re-sending the invoice with a covering note as a first step. This is also a face-saver: it allows your customer to deal with the issue by blaming the accounts department, or the post boy, even if it had nothing to do with them.

Late payment could also represent a fairly unsubtle way of telling you that the service you provided was not particularly special. Your invoice will merely remind the buyer of this fact, and will give him the ultimate sanction. That's why it is so important to use your communication skills up to and beyond the day on which you send out the invoice. At the end of an assignment, I normally ring my client and ask them how they felt it went. We have a friendly chat, and I wait for them to suggest that now would be a good time to send my invoice. There is nothing ill-mannered in getting your invoice in front of the client promptly: it demonstrates that you are efficient, and it also shows the importance you attach to the financial side of the transaction. Clearly, if you are in a mass supply business, you may only be willing to produce invoices on a cycle, rather than individually, but make sure that your satisfied client doesn't have to wait too long before they see the bill. The longer they have to wait, the more the memory fades of the excellent service you provided to them, and the lower the priority the invoice will receive.

You may be forced to re-do work if the buyer simply won't pay. This is an inevitable part of life: some buyers will not be satisfied unless they feel they are getting the better of you, and it happens more often than you might think. You're asked to do work that falls outside of the scope of the original deal, or the end-product you deliver is rejected. You have two alternatives: grit your teeth, do the work, and vow never to deal with the client again; or make a stand and refuse politely unless you are compensated. Neither is a very healthy option: by doing additional work for no extra money, you are breaking one of the first rules of commerce, but by saying no, you are breaking another one. Each case must be judged on its merits: do you want to maintain a relationship with this client? What will the ramifications be if you say no? What do you stand to lose if you have to do more work, and how will that affect assignments with other customers?

Legal action – or the very mention of it – is definitely a last resort, when all else has failed and the relationship is irretrievable. Use your accountant as an adviser here: they will know the right lawyers for the job, and may still be able to suggest less draconian alternatives. You may even decide simply to write off the debt and put it down to experience. Even if it costs you money, it's a lot less trouble than chasing someone who is determined to avoid payment.

Alone and Lonely

As if money problems were not enough, you are going to run up against other issues in this exciting world of commerce. Being on your own can be very lonely, especially when things aren't going well. Loneliness is often a big factor: you miss the workplace, the idle chats by the coffee machine, the noise of an office rumbling around you. The best way to combat loneliness is by being fully occupied: make phone calls, go and visit people, catch up on your administration and keep the business humming. Don't disengage yourself from the rest of the world just because you've chosen a different path to them. Keep in touch with friends and contacts, and make sure you're completely up-to-date with what's happening out there in your chosen market place.

Taking a Breather

Overwork is another potential problem, and it's closely related to loneliness. When you work for an employer, you have a set pattern: you get on the train, arrive at the office, have a gossip over a coffee and then begin your day's tasks. At some stage you will leave the office and go home, making a clear distinction between your two separate lives. During the working day you will have several breaks, either for sustenance or simply to talk to colleagues. A time-and-motion expert could probably estimate how much of your time is spent on non-work activities in the office, and I would guess it runs into hours every day.

But, once you're on your own, all that changes. For a start your office may be in your home, possibly no more than a dozen paces from your bedroom. You can roll out of bed at six-thirty and, still in your pyjamas or nightdress, sit at your desk and do some work. Unshaven, no make-up, but who cares? No one is forcing you to adopt the routines or conventions of big business; no one is watching you. If there's nothing interesting on the television, you can go back into your office in the evening and check for faxes or phone messages, write a report, catch up on your filing, or busy yourself with all those papers that seem to lie permanently in the bottom of your in-tray.

If you stop to add up all the time you spend on work, it is frightening. Your workplace assumes a huge role in your life, and you feel compelled to be in it. From nine to five you can work almost non-stop: no one is going to breeze over for a chat, you don't have to attend interminable internal meetings, and memos will not clog up your desk. Only your customers and suppliers will interrupt your workflow. Before you know where you are, you are becoming a workaholic. I can almost hear you snort in ridicule at the very idea, but I promise you that it happens to the vast majority of sole traders.

Don't be fooled into thinking that a separate office, away from home, will improve matters. Not only is office space expensive, but it can end up being an enormous emotional burden. You feel duty-bound to use it as much as you can but, if you're trading successfully, it will simply become a convenient place to hang your hat and file your papers. During most of the day you won't be in it – you'll be out prospecting or completing assignments – but you'll want to get back to it and read your mail and justify the rent you're paying.

How do you combat overwork? Should you try? Only you can tell whether you're working too hard: if you're married, your partner may well point it out to you, but you have to strike the balance between doing what is necessary to sustain yourself and your dependants and completely ignoring the fact that there is life outside business. Take breaks during the day – even a walk down to the post office or bank is helpful. Get a dog, and commit to walk it every day. On these walks, you get a different perspective on life, away from the immediacy of the office. In Edward's case study, he decided on a completely different strategy whilst walking the dog. Don't eat lunch at your desk: go into kitchen, make yourself a sandwich, turn on the radio or read the newspaper, and enjoy your post-prandial coffee. You have to make an effort to stop the incessant flow of work, otherwise it will consume you and you'll end up in a rubber room.

PIPELINE

Infuriatingly, some of the most horrid management jargon is also the best at describing business functions. 'Pipeline management' is one such phrase, sounding like something they do at BP or Shell, but actually used to describe the process by which sales people manage their portfolio of suspects and prospects.

At the beginning of your reincarnation as a sole trader, you're interested in only one thing: getting a paying customer. All else is subsidiary to this main objective, and nothing can beat the feeling of achieving it. You should never become complacent about your ability to bring in new business, or the buzz it gives you. It is your very *raison d'être*. But you will have to manage the correlation between the number of live customers and the backlog of potential clients. This is what pipeline management is all about.

You reason, not surprisingly, that the more customers you have the better it will be for you. It is undoubtedly healthy to have a diverse group of clients: it spreads the risk, reducing your reliance on a single customer that may suddenly go elsewhere, makes your life more interesting, and puts your name and service in front of wider audience that can then pass it on to others. But you can have too many clients: in effect, you can overtrade, and it's very difficult to know when you're doing it.

Time and Motion

The first way of avoiding overtrading is to look at your available time. Management consultants, as an example, might assume that they have 200 working days in the year. This takes into account holidays, illness, doctor and dentist appointments, little Johnny's sports day, and other such activities. Of those 200 days, a consultant will estimate how many will be fee-paying, and very few assume that the number will be greater than 50 per cent: in reality, it's likely to be a lot less. That's roughly how a consultant, who is selling nothing but time and expertise, estimates cost and price. But it's also useful because it allows the consultant to judge how many clients could be effectively serviced in a year. If the consultant assumes that at least 100 days will be consumed by business development, administration and relationship manage-ment, it leaves 100 days for assignments. If the average assignment lasts 20 man-days, then the consultant cannot take on more than five customers every year.

Of course, it doesn't work out like that in the real world, but it's a good place to start. Determine how much time you can devote to direct revenue activity, and you'll be much less likely to take on too much work. Workflow planning is a necessarily imprecise science: very inconveniently, assignments aren't given when you're expecting them and, like the number 19 bus, you can wait ages for one to arrive and then three come in a row.

What can possibly be wrong with overtrading, you might ask? Surely the more business I bring in the better? Yes and no. Remember that, as a sole trader, you are highly dependent for your continued success on the quality of service you deliver to your clients. If you have too many, it follows that some of them will not receive the full attention they deserve and are paying for. Much better to have a smaller group of wholly satisfied customers who will come back to you again and again, than to have lots of clients who pay you only once.

Looking down the Barrel

As part of the process of pipeline management, you must worry about what might come up in the future – you must put your eye to the end of the pipeline and look down it to see what's approaching. Airlines have got this down to a fine art: they routinely overbook every flight they can, because they know that there will be no-shows and cancellations. In the same way, it is sensible to do a little bit of overbooking yourself: you should always be talking to many more suspects and prospects than you can possibly handle, because they won't all sign up with you. In my experience, probably no more than 10 per cent of the people I sell to actually end up buying my products: maybe 50 per cent of suspects become prospects, and a fifth of those actually sign the contract. As you become more skilful at selling, and more discriminating in your targeting of prospects, this ratio increases: you should also bear in mind that you won't have to sell yourself to existing clients if you've done a good job for them, because they'll always come back for more.

The pipeline, especially for those products and services that are relatively expensive and take a long time to sell, is an extremely important element in the management and planning of your business. If you have the balance right, you will never need to worry about what you will be doing when the current work runs out: there will always be something on the horizon. Your long-term aim is to build a business base that is self-generating, so that clients come back for more without you having to cold-call on new suspects. But the prudent sole trader is always looking down that pipeline, and will feed the other end if it looks empty.

PARTNERSHIPS

If you've managed to get this far in the book, but you've yet to be convinced that the life of the sole trader is for you, you may be wondering whether a partnership is really what you need. Maybe you have a friend who is also looking to change direction; maybe someone at work wants to go into business with you; or you may simply be hesitant about the idea of striking out on your own, and taking on all the trials and tribulations of the micro-entrepreneur single-handed.

Fear, Uncertainty and Doubt – The FUD Factor

On paper, a partnership looks like a very good idea. When you analyse your strengths and weaknesses you will undoubtedly find holes in your armoury, areas where you feel less than confident. Having someone else by your side, someone who can brings skills to the table that you don't have, would solve a lot of your problems. That, at least, is the theory and, to a limited extent, it is correct: many of the problems most frequently encountered by sole traders are related to their concerns over a lack of experience. You've never sold before; you're no good with money; you don't know how to manage suppliers; the list goes on. Finding a partner with complementary skills would help you to focus and concentrate on what you are good at.

Sometimes partnerships work out exactly like that, with the principals fulfilling different roles that don't overlap: they agree on the overall strategy of the business, and execute the tactics according to their talents. More often, however, partnerships don't quite work out that way. Why not?

If you have a desire to be your own boss, and control your own destiny, you are going to have to be absolutely determined and committed. You will need to fight your way through the bad times, keep your head in times of crisis, and satisfy the requirements and aspirations of any dependents, following your chosen path through thick and thin. You'll need to be flexible and adaptable, changing course when unexpected opportunities arise, and you'll have to devote more time and effort than you ever imagined just to keep all the balls in the air. Many of the people interviewed in the case studies talked about their previous lives as employees, and one of the strands running through their discussions was their impatience with the way in which colleagues behaved – the general consensus appeared to be that others did not live up to their expectations. That's hardly surprising: most of the case-study individuals have gone on to be highly successful sole traders, validating their self-belief and high standards.

The acquisition of a partner can recall all the horrors of working with and for other people. Inevitably there will be differences of opinion about the way in which a business is run. As an employee, you have to toe the company line but, as a sole trader, you can do what you want, and follow your instincts. Adding another factor to the equation limits your scope for this, whatever the benefits may be. When partners disagree, there's bound to be friction and resentment, and unwinding a partnership can be soul-destroying and expensive. You have to ask yourself the fundamental question: can I do this thing on my own? If the answer is yes, adding a partner makes no sense.

Not Quite Partners

Much better, therefore, to consider the alternatives that still keep you in overall control but allow you to call upon the expertise of others. As mentioned in an earlier chapter, there are whole armies of individuals and companies ready and waiting to take on jobs that you either don't want to do, or can't do. Outsourcing parts of your operation to specialists is a simple way of clearing your desk of all the unimportant clutter, without having to give away part of the business to achieve it.

There are more formal arrangements to be considered that allow you to make money and keep control. For instance, you can set up agreements with other businesses to cross-refer opportunities, in return for a percentage of any revenue earnt. You may wonder how you make contact with these businesses. The answer is, you network like crazy. As you start up on your own, you'll be amazed at how often you bump in to other sole traders – it's like the time when you have your first baby and, almost imperceptibly, all your friends suddenly have babies as well. One formal method of doing this is by looking at the trade associations and local business organizations that might prove useful to you. It seems that nowadays every industry has at least one trade association, and most run open evenings where you can turn up and look at how they operate, the services they provide, and talk to the other members. You can also go to your local chamber of commerce and see if there's anything interesting there for you. And you shouldn't rule out the possibility of joining a more generic type of organization, like the Institute of Directors, which offers facilities that you'll be unlikely to find anywhere else.

This networking can lead to alliances, rather than partnerships; you agree with another business to do some work together, or to pass on referrals, without going through the tortuous and time-consuming process of a more formal consolidation. If things don't work out, you've lost very little, but if they go well, you may end up making some extra money and you will be keeping your customers satisfied.

When considering any type of accommodation or arrangement with another party, you have to keep in mind two essential issues. Firstly, you need to be sure that there is some benefit in it for you, and that it will not diminish or inhibit your freedom to act as you wish. Secondly, you want to ensure that the ultimate objective, of providing the best possible service to your customers, is either protected or enhanced by the alliance. If either of these pre-conditions fails to be met, you should walk away from the opportunity.

POTENTIAL

What is a business for? There are numerous altruistic and selfish motives for running a business, large or small, but ultimately it has to provide some benefit to the people running and owning it by satisfying a market need. If that sounds like a bit of a truism, you need only look at the number of high-profile businesses, and whole industries, in the UK that have failed simply because they no longer understood it. Nowadays it is fashionable to talk about stakeholders in a business – the shareholders, employees, customers and suppliers – all of whom have an interest in seeing that business prosper and grow. As a sole trader, you represent 50 per cent of the stakeholders – so it's only natural that you should put your own priorities at the top of the list when it comes to considering the rationale for continuing to run the operation.

Potential and Reality

But it's easy to fall into a rut, to believe that because you are satisfying market demand today, and keeping yourself in baked beans and beer, that nothing much needs to change other than the occasional redesign of your stationery or the purchase of a better word processor. You can plan for these things, for increasing expenditure and revenue, because you know they will occur at some stage. But looking at the potential of your business is altogether a different proposition.

The question you must be asking yourself on a regular basis is this: what is the potential for my business, and for me? Potential is that part of your constitution that you can dream about, and dreaming is no bad thing, in moderation. You want to consider how things might turn out and how you would react to them. For example, if you were approached by a customer or a supplier who had decided to buy you out, and offered you a lot of money for the privilege, what would you do? Does your business have the potential for this to happen? If not, should that concern you?

Large organizations have product management and development functions, as well as eggheads who think about strategy and the long-term future of the world as it relates to their company. Economists predict global and local trends, marketing gurus pontificate on the next likely hot buttons. Little you, with no one so erudite to turn to, have to rely on yourself to determine how your business will fit in to the world order. In the back of your mind you should have an idea of your earnings plateau or ceiling, the maximum revenue figure you're ever likely to reach if you were permanently fully employed by your customers. That figure should always be much higher than the amount you think you can survive on, and the amount you're currently earning. If it isn't, you're going to have a serious problem, because the potential for your business to grow is limited from the moment you set up.

Of course, in your plans you expect that the business will take off and show considerable growth after the anxious early days. For most of the people featured in the case studies, this is what has happened. But a common theme in interviews with them was that they were all wondering about how to maximize the effectiveness of their business, how to squeeze the most they could out of their working days. Not one case study suggested that they would end up as mega-rich as a result of their own efforts, and neither did they articulate this as a major ambition. But they are all striving to reach a combination of job satisfaction and adequate earnings so that their efforts are seen by themselves, and their dependants, as being worthwhile.

You as the Personnel Director

That's what potential is all about. Most of us soon realize that what we are doing today is only a fraction of what we might achieve, given half a chance and the right circumstances. We are merely scratching the surface of the business and the demand that is currently out there, and we want to tap into it more deeply. Each one of the case-study interviewees was deeply concerned about the quality of work they undertook, and the value placed on it by their customers. They want buyers to keep coming back for more, and not necessarily more of the same; one interviewee said that she would feel rather foolish if she were still doing exactly the same job in 10 years' time. She, and many others like her, doesn't fear failure nearly as much as she fears the idea of becoming stale, or not having tried to do something different, more challenging or rewarding. That is what would make her feel foolish – that her customers didn't realize all the other things she could do.

So what is your potential? As an employee, we get used to the notion that we are specialists in a particular field, and that we have to call in other specialists when our work falls outside that field. This is patently incorrect, as well as being the most

obnoxious form of career management – 'He works in the finance
department, so he'd never make it as a salesman' – because the
majority of us are itching to try our hands at something else.
Personnel managers rarely accept that staff will rise to a new
challenge, and will take great pride in being given the opportunity
to try something new. Instead they want to pigeon-hole every-
body, not only because the personnel filing system is much easier
to manage if they do but also because they perceive there is less
risk involved if they keep people in functions where they've
already proved their ability. A good example of this comes from
the sales environment: it is almost legendary that the best sales
people make the worst sales managers, and yet that is the route
they are forced to take. If only personnel managers could apply a
bit of lateral thinking there wouldn't be so many duff sales
managers around.

As a sole trader, however, you are the Human Resources
Director. You, and only you, have the opportunity to pat yourself
on the back and say, 'Well, Buggins, it's time for a bigger/
different/riskier job. Let's see how you get on.' A fair few sole
traders do exactly that, and many larger entrepreneurs as well,
and turn their next venture into just as much of a success as the
first one. Just because you've started out with one idea in mind
doesn't mean that you have to be slavishly devoted to it for the
rest of your working days. And, whilst the majority of us tend to
evolve gradually into new opportunities, some people make an
absolute break with the past and try their luck in a completely
different market.

A Wealth of Experience

What you will undoubtedly overlook, unless you happen to be
extremely self-assured, is that your experience as a sole trader
qualifies you to do almost anything within reason. I'm not
suggesting that you switch from being a potter to a brain
surgeon, but you probably get the general idea. You'll acquire

financial management skills, sales expertise, product-management experience, customer-relations knowledge, as well as the determination and appetite for hard work that only the successful sole trader possesses. Who knows what you could do with all this high-level managerial experience? That's potential – the trick for you, as for every other micro-entrepreneur, is knowing how to exploit it and translate it into reality.

Chapter Eight

NOTHING LASTS FOREVER

'The best laid plans o' mice an' men
Gang aft a-gley.'
Robert Burns, 1786

'Anything that can go wrong will go wrong.'
Murphy's Law

No one would ever think of going into business for themselves unless they were entirely convinced that their plans had merit, and that the enterprise would ultimately be successful. If you've managed to read all the previous chapters you'll already have some idea of how arduous the road to success can be, and of the strength, determination and sheer bloody-mindedness that you need to make a go of it. I like to believe that the optimism within oneself when starting up as a sole trader continues to flourish, even if it becomes tinged with a little realism in the light of experience.

But you have to know when enough is enough, when there is simply no alternative to grasping your head in despair and throwing in the towel. Although the purpose of this book is to inspire you to become a master or mistress of your own destiny, and break free of the shackles of employment, it is only fair to point out that a large proportion of sole traders ultimately fail to achieve what they hoped to when they started. The grand schemes and plans that they put in place simply don't come to fruition. Sometimes they are prepared to accept this, and adjust their lives to take account of the diminished potential that self-employment offers as a result. More often, however, they decide that the benefits of freedom simply don't outweigh the drawbacks of hard slog for too little money, and they return to the great corporate market place in search of a job.

On a more positive note, many successful sole traders find that they make themselves the target of much wooing and seduction by employers eager to use their skills on a more permanent basis. Especially where you are adding true value to a customer's operations – say as a consultant or an adviser – that company will recognize your skills and expertise and will inevitably question the long-term sense of paying your fees without gaining some measure of exclusivity. In such cases, many companies will make an offer that simply cannot be refused – or, at the very least, that must be seriously considered.

Whatever the circumstances, it has to be accepted that being your own boss is not a one-way street. You may well find that a return to employment is the best option for future development and growth, and this shouldn't frighten you. As a sole trader, your mind should constantly be open to the prospect of fresh challenges and opportunities, however they present themselves.

Are You Really Unemployable?

Every successful sole trader will tell you that they have become so independent as to be virtually unemployable, and there is a strong element of truth in this. You get so used to the situation where you make all the decisions, take all the risks, manage all the functions, and are seemingly answerable to no one but your clients, that you begin to believe that you could never take orders from anyone else, that no one could possibly have the necessary skills that you've picked up, or be able to deal with you in a reasonable and grown-up manner.

This belief, however, has to be challenged, and challenged regularly. You have to look at things from the opposite perspective before you can make any decisions about whether a return to employment is really out of the question. For those of us who have made the break, and run our own business, there is often a feeling of great surprise and pride in the fact that we have managed on our own, that we have adapted to a completely new regime and environment, and that we have simply made things happen. We are particularly pleased with ourselves when we try something new and it works; we may even take a little pride in the effort of doing this, even if things don't work out quite so well. What I'm getting at is that the sole trader is forced to take risks, to be adaptable, and to turn their hand to whatever it is that will make them most money and give them the greatest satisfaction.

So, having achieved all this, shouldn't sole traders also have that necessary flexibility to assimilate themselves back into an employer/employee relationship? Of course they should, but no one likes to accept this: there is so much kudos attached to the idea of making a living solely from your own efforts that you find it slightly odious to consider that you could be just as valuable, and have just as much self-esteem, if you were working for someone else.

Pride in your work is an admirable, and vital, constituent for the sole trader. But you also build up a pride in yourself, a feeling of self-confidence, so that you begin to feel that no one else in the world could possibly do things as well as you do. This manifests itself in the attitude of sole traders towards a return to employment – look at all the case studies and see how many of them claim that they don't feel they could ever work for anyone else. But this attitude comes from the very same people who will never say never, who will judge each opportunity on its merits and analyse each opportunity rationally and prudently.

Learning to come to terms with your own fallibility and weaknesses is hard. It is especially hard for those of us who have made a real success of our lives as micro-entrepreneurs, and who cannot conceive of a life where someone else in charge, and in which we may no longer have the premium of knowledge, wisdom and experience. Whilst we may be prepared to accept that accountants know more than we do about tax, there are very few other people in whom we have as much confidence as ourselves.

This very self-confidence, however, is exactly what is needed if you are ever considering returning to work as an employee. The poise that you have developed, the skills you have acquired, the focus and determination you have honed, are all attributes that major companies are crying out for. In a previous chapter I mentioned that big companies are trying to behave like small companies, trying to introduce the entrepreneurial spirit that is so sadly lacking in most organizations. Big employers are realizing that they must give more autonomy to independent business units, not only because it makes economic sense but also because it motivates the staff more effectively – and motivated staff are happy staff.

Think about it – you shouldn't start your own business with the hard-and-fast rule that you're never going to go back to being an employee. Life isn't like that – nothing lasts forever and, when and if the time comes and the opportunity looks right, you must consider it with an open mind. Only you set the rules and monitor your compliance with them, and only you can judge success and failure. Big Brother isn't watching you: you can do what you like, and if that means changing course completely, then you only need satisfy yourself and your dependants that it's the right thing to do.

What Went Wrong?

Small businesses fail in droves every day. Nowadays there isn't even much of a stigma attached to bankruptcy. It has become so common that many people regard it simply as a nasty hiccup, and are quite willing to help you pick yourself up, dust yourself down, and start all over again. Obviously no one likes to see a business fail, especially a small one; suppliers worry that they won't get paid, and about the domino effect this will have on them and their suppliers. But failure is treated with much less suspicion that it used to be. This is really an American trend, where bankruptcies have always been commonplace and the law caters for it in a way that protects sick companies from their creditors. The Americans cherish and reward their pioneers – ''Tis better to have fought and lost than never to have fought at all' – and love nothing more than the story of a loser who eventually wins. I think that the motto of every sole trader should simply be 'Try!'

But many sole traders will try, and will not succeed. This can be for numerous reasons: the business plan was flawed, the product never met customer expectations, the opportunity disappeared before there was a chance to fill it, the cash inflows and outflows never matched, the competition was too fierce or, more prosaically, the sole trader just couldn't deal with all the independence and the responsibilities that come with it. There's really no single over-riding reason for failure, although I suspect that cashflow features pretty high on the list of probable causes. The questions that really need to be answered are these: when do I know that my business is a failure, and how do I untangle myself from it?

Bowing out Gracefully

All failure is relative. For the sole trader, failure has to judged in purely personal terms. Does my business meet the aspirations I originally had when I started out? Is it ever likely to, or have my aspirations changed to such an extent that the existing business can no longer support them? Am I happy and, if not now, will I ever be doing what I'm doing? What strains has self-employment put on my relationships with my spouse/partner/children/others? Has the quality of my life improved or deteriorated as a result of my decision to go it alone? Do I miss the security blanket of having an employer, with all the attendant perks? Those of us blessed with a modicum of success will rarely stand back and ask these hard questions, either because we're too frightened or because we think we already know the answers. But all sole traders should periodically examine themselves, their motivations and aspirations, and the direction of their business and personal lives, to see if being on their own remains the brilliant idea it was when they started.

If the answers to these questions are negative, you need to take action very swiftly to put things right. There's no point sitting around moping because your business hasn't taken off – sulking about it achieves nothing. Instead you must draw on all the reserves of ingenuity that you have built up as an independent operator to consider how you're going to deal with your problem. You will have to think about four options: selling out, transferring, closing down, or a complete relaunch.

A Going Concern?

Far be it from me, a complete no-hoper when it comes to accountancy, to tell you how to judge whether you have a saleable business. You are most likely in the same situation, especially if you are really offering a service rather than a tangible product. But don't discount the idea that someone else might be very interested in your client list, and could well pay you a little something to take them off your hands. Practically speaking, this happens all too rarely, mainly because the sole trader has no idea of who might be interested and no way of finding out. But if you deal with an accounting firm that handles other small businesses, you may find that they can identify a buyer – for a commission, naturally. Sometimes, if you're very lucky, you may meet a natural buyer through your network of contacts, but you will still need to get an accountant, and quite possibly a lawyer, involved to handle all the details.

Transfer Market Activity

The problem with selling a business that relies almost exclusively on service is that you are the service, and what is most attractive to potential buyers is the prospect of you continuing to run the relationships with your buyers. The last thing they want is to be left with a group of customers they know nothing about, and vice versa. So many sole traders find that the best compromise is to transfer their business, and themselves, to another company; the luckiest ones end up with some kind of partnership deal, and guarantees of a certain amount of independence post-merger. Companies place a lot of value on the acquisition of warm clients, but only if they have the assurance that they will continue to stay warm.

Close of Play

Horrific as it may sound, closing the business down may be the most practical solution to the problem. Perhaps you have become too proprietorial to consider a sale or transfer, or maybe you're so depressed that the thought of continuing to function in the same market, under whatever circumstances, is too grim to contemplate. If these conditions apply, or your customer base is so lousy that nobody in their right mind would want to pay for it, then you probably have no alternative. The less said about this the better – it's something we don't want to dwell on in a book like this!

The Phoenix Rises

OK, so you messed things up. You misread the market, you didn't do your homework, your USPs all turned out to be turkeys, and the money went out a lot faster than it came in. That should have taught you quite a lot – in fact, many successful entrepreneurs would claim that they learn much more from failure than success. What's to stop you having another go? As long as your creditors let you, there's no reason why you shouldn't try again, better armed with your first-hand knowledge of all the pitfalls and set-backs that can kill a small business. Every year thousands of products come to the market and fail, but producers go back to the drawing board and relaunch them with better features and benefits or ditch them as hopeless. But they learn from their mistakes, if they are going to continue in business. So can you.

A relaunch can be just that: you can take the same product or service and, with a different marketing approach and sales technique, you can have much greater success. The telephone-based banking service of Midland, First Direct, illustrates the point: the marketing gurus believed that phone banking would appeal to the younger generation, and pitched the product accordingly. To their great surprise it transpired that the majority of new clients came from a much older – and more affluent – market sector. So you no longer see the wacky commercials on television, or the strange posters, because the marketing department has accepted that the product appeals to a different and more lucrative audience, and have adjusted their strategy accordingly.

In the same way, you may find that you simply missed your target market: you thought your service would appeal to a certain constituency but it didn't. As long as you know why, and how to get to the right market, there's nothing to stop you going back in with a relaunch.

A relaunch could go much further: you might want to alter

the features so that they offer different or improved benefits, which you may have learnt from experience are more likely to prove attractive to buyers. And there's nothing to stop you copying the winners – if you can understand how competitors do well, you can adapt their ideas, customize them for your buyers, and come up with a better mousetrap, even if it's not the best. Just make sure you don't infringe any patents or copyrights.

Communications – Again!

Whichever strategy you choose, your customers have to know about it. But you should really be in a position to discuss your future with your clients before deciding on what to do. Your best clients are your partners, people who have a vested interest in seeing you succeed, and they will be only too happy to offer you their advice and counsel. I have frequently been to talk to my major customers about the direction of my business, what they feel I should be offering them as additional services, and how I can best meet their future requirements. If you have built a good relationship with your customers, they should be a major source of assistance when it comes to point where you feel a radical overhaul is needed.

Not all your customers, however, are going to be interested in your long-term strategy. They will only be concerned with whether you can finish existing assignments on time and to budget and specification, so you need to reassure them that you will continue to offer the same levels of professionalism as always, even if you are going to wind the business up once the work is complete.

This maintenance of standards, right up until the moment you shut up shop for the last time, is desperately important. You never know when you might need your customers again: they may reappear as potential employers, for example, or you may decide to go into business for yourself at some later stage and discover that you're still having to deal with some of your former buyers. Don't burn your bridges by letting standards drop.

Adieu, Administrivia

Possibly the most painful part of accepting defeat is having to go through exactly the same process as you did when you started out with all your dreams and aspirations intact. All the people and institutions that you contacted to herald the arrival of a brave new business will also be interested in knowing that it is coming to an end – the tax and VAT men, the stationery supplier, the utilities companies, the bank, all those annoying distractions that seemed to add nothing to your well-being and general wealth. Almost certainly you will have outstanding financial commitments that you will need to take into account when calculating the cost of accepting defeat. It is soul-destroying to have to write and say that you're no longer in business, but it must be done quickly and efficiently. Make a clean break, learn your lessons well, and then get motivated for the future.

Nothing Lasts Forever

The great excitement about life as a sole trader is that the future is entirely in your hands. You can chop and change product and service at will, as long as they continue to add value to your customers, and you can determine at what point you need to change direction. In the back of every micro-entrepreneur's mind is the implicit realization that next year will not be the same as last year, that they will develop and grow as an individual and a professional, and that unknown forces will push them into new and uncharted waters. That's what is so stimulating about the whole process of working for yourself. If I were challenged to identify the one quality above all others that is needed to make a success of life as a sole trader, that quality would be pragmatism.

Nothing is carved in stone, and nothing lasts forever – the best of the self-employed adapt and change like chameleons, always in harmony with their surroundings.

Sole traders don't look back; they don't dwell on past failures; they don't have the time to spend on memories of what went before. If you reach the stage where the business has failed to achieve what you hoped it might, you must take decisive action and, in precisely the same way as you mapped out the future when you made your plans at the start, you must look ahead with the same degree of optimism and excitement. For some people, being a sole trader might have been forced upon them, and that experience will have greatly added to their overall worth. It really doesn't matter whether you are a sole trader for five or fifty years: what is more important is that you tried it. Millions of people never have the opportunity to find out if they can make it on their own or not – the lucky few that do rarely regret the experience, however harrowing it might seem at the time.

Chapter Nine

CASE STUDIES

Maggie the Literary Agent

Literary agents have a tough job. They act as brokers between authors and publishers, selling books either as complete manuscripts or at the idea stage as synopses, and then negotiating the financial and contractual arrangements on behalf of writers in return for a percentage of their earnings. They must be both sensitive and hard-nosed, stroking the delicate egos of writers whilst ensuring that they get the best possible deal from the publisher. They have to be able to separate work of merit from dross, and undertake much work for nothing – they only get paid for results. As a result, they end up caught between the conflicting demands of both sides of the writing relationship, and must therefore be consummate sales and relationship managers.

Maggie started her career as secretary to a director of a large literary agency – 'the worst secretary they'd ever had,' so she believes. Whether she had secretarial skills or not, by the age of 21 she was in charge of the foreign-rights department, negotiating overseas publishing contracts for authors. In time she was allowed to expand her activities and to represent a portfolio of 6 young science-fiction writers for whom she started selling UK publishing rights, and expanded that to 12.

Just as her career appeared to be taking off, she was struck down with ME, long before it became a fashionable disease, and was unable to work. After six months of suffering, she was issued with an ultimatum by her employer – either she came back to work full-time or not at all. Unable to comply, she left them, still unwell, but managed to work one day a week as a freelance for another agency. With no clients, and only a small income from family money, in 1981 she decided to take the plunge and strike out on her own. With the economy in recession, the big agencies were not taking on any new clients, which she hoped would work to her advantage. She went through her address book and sent out a printed business card to everyone she knew, announcing her new agency. A friend of hers who was an agent gave her good initial advice: try to sell non-fiction books first, as these are often bought on the basis of a synopsis, which means that an advance is paid before the book is written.

Maggie deliberately avoided approaching former clients from her ex-employer, but authors came to her. Her philosophy in those early days was straightforward: 'I wanted to try and succeed but, if it didn't work out, I knew I could get another job.' Her bank manager was very understanding, and gave her advice on accounting for income and expenditure, and she also consulted with her former boss who had retired from the agency. 'I thought about the idea of a partnership,' Maggie says, 'but there simply wasn't enough money coming in to support more than one person. I also wanted to work from home, which would have been more difficult.' She soon realized that she would need a lot of help from other people: 'Accounting frightened me,' she says, 'so I used a royalty accountant whom I knew from my old agency, and hired an accountant who understood the book trade.'

Maggie admits that she missed the gossip of the old agency, and the comfort of having a big name to back her up. The early days were lonely: 'I used to save up my photocopying and take it down to the local estate agents, who'd very kindly allowed me to use their machine, so at least I had some face-to-face contact.' But she didn't miss office politics, and found herself becoming much more productive: 'I didn't have to deal with internal issues, and could work at hours to suit myself.'

Eventually, having proved to herself and others that she could handle a wide range of books, Maggie took on science-fiction and fantasy writers, an area where she had already developed an expertise. 'Very few agents handle that genre, and it is a lucrative part of my list. There's a constant renewal of readership.' But other areas present more of a problem, and this is where strong business sense also plays a part: 'Unfortunately, well-written novels don't pay the bills,' she maintains. 'I handle a lot of big fat novels for big fat ladies.' She also has travel, history, biography, leisure, popular psychology and children's titles on her list.

Maggie is a member of the Association of Authors' Agents, the main trade body, but she also set up an informal group of independent agents who meet regularly to swap war stories and share the frustrations and trials common to every agent.

'Stroking writers is a very important part of the job,' Maggie says. 'There's lots of phone contact. I see my role as a mixture of nanny, psychologist, financial adviser and sales person.' Maggie sticks to a rule that she developed whilst working at the large agency: 'I never take on a client that I wouldn't want to give my home phone number to.' Writers, who can be very tiresome and whose books are difficult to sell, tend to ring at all hours.

'You have to have the right temperament if you're going to succeed on your own,' Maggie maintains. 'It's also important to learn to delegate, and find the right people to work with.' Maggie now employs a small group of helpers: 'A huge amount of my income goes on salaries,' she says, 'but using other people allows me to do the things I want to do.' Top of the list of priorities is her small daughter, with whom Maggie wants to spend as much time as possible, though not to the detriment of her authors.

For the future, Maggie is enthusiastically investigating the new technology, such as CD-I and CD-ROM, that is gaining pace in the publishing world. But she thinks there will always be a market for the written word: 'When television arrived, many predicted the death of reading, but it didn't happen. Technology will complement, but not replace, books.' And does she think she'll ever return to the corporate world? 'Now that I've been my own boss, I think I'm unemployable,' she says frankly, and a little defiantly.

Edward the Researcher

Having joined an American bank in 1973, Edward worked his way up the corporate ladder – including a spell in Sydney as operations manager for a large US financial institution – until he was made redundant in 1990. 'At the time,' he says, 'I was given outplacement counselling, which was useful because it made me think about what I wanted to do and how I was going to achieve it.' He had long considered the prospect of going into business for himself but, 'I just couldn't come up with the Big Idea. So I reluctantly took another job.' Within two years, he had been made redundant again, and was given a reasonable settlement by his employer.

'I knew that this was the right time to do it,' Edward says. 'I was much better prepared for the cultural leap. The family was on holiday in Devon, and I drove back down after being fired and talked it all through with my wife. Initially, I wanted to settle down in Devon and do something from there, but my wife very sensibly argued that this was impractical, at least until I'd got the business established.' Edward used the techniques he'd learnt from his previous counselling to decide what he was going to, and calculated that he had 10 months to get the business up and running – that was how long the redundancy money would last. But things didn't work out quite how he'd planned: 'After 6 months, there was still no business coming in and we were seriously concerned. I'd decided that the best route was to sell my consulting services back to my former employers, and I'd chosen an area where I thought there would be a lot of interest.'

Fretting over his initial lack of success, Edward took the dog for a long walk one day and reconsidered all his plans. 'I thought about what I'd wanted when I was a buyer of consultancy services at the various banks I'd worked for. Doing that gave me a much better idea of what the market was really looking for.' Suitably invigorated, Edward came back and drew up a new business plan, and within six weeks the first project was live, with paying customers. 'As a buyer, I'd always been frustrated by the lack of high-quality research and marketing advice,' Edward recalls, 'so I decided to tap in to that area.' This was a bold move: he was taking on some well-established major players in the financial research industry, but he used his contacts well and identified their needs through applying his own experience to their situation.

'The first 10 months went very well,' he remembers. He sold research projects to former employers and his name began to get recognition in the market. But he was too focused on the business he was carrying out, failing to look far enough ahead. 'I concentrated too much on one product, and kept on trotting out the same old ideas. I needed to have more irons in the fire.' Additionally, he suffered from the capricious nature of customers: 'They would tell me they wanted a particular type of research,' he says, 'and I'd go away and do the groundwork, only to discover that they'd changed their minds in the interim, and I wasn't able to sell the project to anyone.'

When he started, Edward bought a big set of index cards and wrote down the names and numbers of all the contacts he'd built up over 19 years in the banking industry. 'From time to time I go back to those cards and give them a call, just to keep my name in front of them.' He took advice initially from an executive-search consultant who gave him guidance on how to price short-term assignments, and won his very first piece of business from another consultant who was looking to sub-contract part of a deal he had won.

'My wife and family were very supportive, and continue to be so,' Edward says. 'We'd calculated that we could survive on a lot less than I'd been earning as an employee, and the bank was very good to us – although the business has never gone overdrawn. The temptation was to spend all the money I earned in the first year, but we didn't do it. We put money aside: in this business, where money comes in infrequently and you never know when buyers will make a decision, you have to build up a reserve to cover the lean months.'

The priority for Edward now is to expand the scope of his market-research activities: 'Basically, I piece together a lot of different data and ideas to come up with potential opportunities for new research projects.' His estimates of how his time is divided are interesting: 'The main focus of my working day is the promotion of myself, through the use of all the contacts I have,' he says. 'As a result, I probably spend 50 per cent of my time on business promotion and development. The actual research work probably constitutes only 30 per cent of what I do. That's the main piece of advice I'd give to people thinking of setting up on their own: don't forget the importance of business promotion.'

On the Big Idea, Edward is pragmatic: 'It doesn't need to be a revolutionary idea, which is the mistake I originally made. But whatever you do must be well-delivered and must give customers something they can't get from anyone else.' Edward now spends much of his time on business planning: 'Unlike the early days, when I was simply concerned with signing up clients, I've now lengthened my planning horizons,' he says. 'I worry about where the money is going to come from in 18 to 24 months, so planning is absolutely vital.'

Successfully established, Edward still wants to move away from London, but to continue to run the business from home. 'I definitely don't want to go back to the life of an employee,' he says. 'I really enjoy getting up in the morning and starting work, which is a feeling that can't be beaten.'

Simon the Surveyor

Surveyors act as a critical link in the property chain. Amongst many functions, they advise clients on rent and lease renewals, assist in the identification, valuation and acquisition of properties,

work on development opportunities, undertake reviews of regulation and other planning restrictions, manage property assets on
behalf of clients, and offer marketing advice on the sale of
property.

Simon qualified as a chartered surveyor in 1962 and is now a
Fellow of the Royal Institute of Chartered Surveyors. With a
background in property development, in 1968 he joined a large
London-based firm of surveyors where he spent 11 years as an
equity partner. 'I was in the top 10 in the pecking order,' Simon
recalls. But the continuous bickering between the partners took
its toll: 'Internal politics were the main reason for my departure,'
he says. 'I'd set up and run the overseas operation, and had taken
on a lot of responsibilities when I returned to London – research,
computerization, advertising and marketing – as well as managing the office agency business. But the in-fighting was too much,
and I'd reached the point where I just wanted to get out.' At the
time, in 1983, the firm was considering incorporation. The
partners were all hoping for a major windfall from this, and they
wanted to reduce the number of equity partners so that the
remaining few would receive more money.

'I volunteered to leave the partnership,' Simon says, 'and,
after much negotiation, we agreed a financial settlement.' He
estimates, without any hint of regret, that the decision to leave
before incorporation probably cost him about £1 million. 'I'd
made a great investment of heart and soul in the firm,' he says,
'but I was suffering from intellectual boredom. The firm had
become so motivated by profit that nothing else seemed to matter
to the partners.'

Simon's wife was entirely supportive of his decision to leave,
even though he had no idea of what he was going to do. 'I sat in
splendid isolation, wondering how I was going to earn my
living.' But he spurned the idea of going back into another large
firm: 'I was offered a job with the leading firm of surveyors to go
and set up and manage their Singapore office, but I turned it
down. I wanted to prove that I could do something on my own.'

He also did something very unusual: he deliberately avoided trying to take clients away from his old partnership. 'I wanted to leave the firm with a clean pair of hands,' Simon says.

Having written to all his contacts telling them that he was setting up his own practice, Simon was soon introduced to the realities of life as a sole trader. His first job was for his brother-in-law, and it was based on a success fee – if the deal came off, Simon would be paid, otherwise he'd get nothing. 'Eventually the project fell through, after three months of hard work,' he says. 'I got paid my expenses – £98 – and nothing more.' But the letters he had sent out began to produce other business, and the next job he got led to a further 15 or 20 assignments as people began to see how much money he could make or save for them.

'I very quickly changed direction when I realized where the money was,' Simon says. But even today he takes on assignments which may not turn out to be profitable. Nodding at a huge pile of folders, Simon says: 'Mega-deals are rather like doing the pools. There is always the prospect that you'll hit the jackpot.' With his office in the basement of the family home, and a part-time secretary to help him, he has some valuable advice on premises. 'I took serviced offices in the West End, because I was concerned that customers wouldn't take me seriously if I was working from home. But it was really only a West End loo – I never had appointments there, and it was a waste of money. Over the years I've learnt that customers buy the individual, not the premises.'

On the issue of being a one-man band, and competing head-on with large firms, Simon is sanguine. 'I win jobs because my clients know I will do the work effectively, and I'm on call 24 hours a day. I have undoubtedly lost jobs because of the fear that I'll be run over by a bus, but I think that danger is just as real if you're dealing with one partner in a large firm. As long as your files are in order, someone else will be able to pick up where you left off.'

Simon is particularly proud of the time when he represented

a client in court. They were up against one of the major institutions, and they won a landmark case, the court awarding his client costs – which was unheard of in the property business. He feels it taught him an important lesson. 'As a sole trader, it's natural to believe that you have expertise in one specific area, and not others. But, once you're on your own, you have to do all these things, and I've certainly got into areas that I'd never handled before, like the court case. That's intellectually challenging. If you have to sink or swim, you bloody well swim. That's the liberation of doing everything for yourself. Experts in one specific area tend to over-complicate matters unnecessarily.'

For the future, Simon is open-minded. 'I wouldn't be averse to looking at other things,' he says. 'I always go along to interviews: they can give you a good valuation of your own worth, and can act as a great boost to morale. You should never say "never". But it's difficult to see me changing after so much time on my own.' He admits that he has done no sales work since his first letters to his network of contacts. He has had some well-produced brochures printed, but everything else is reliant on contacts. And he uses his trade association for this as well, calling on the expertise of other members when necessary.

What advice would he give to the budding micro-entrepreneur? 'You need to be prepared to earn no money for the first nine months,' Simon believes. 'Everything takes twice as long as you think it will, and the fees never appear when you're expecting them. And you will have to work extremely hard – but the job satisfaction is enormous.' He also admits that setting money aside remains difficult – 'much easier said than done'. Whilst being interviewed, Simon opened the morning post to illustrate the variety of opportunities on offer. 'It's exciting to open the mail every day and not know what you're going to find.'

Anne the Human Resources Consultant

By her own admission, Anne was a late developer. 'I was a non-starter at secondary school,' she admits candidly. Having spent several years as a tourist guide, she finally went to university and came out armed with a degree at the age of 29. With no business experience, she drifted into management consultancy, joining a large firm as one of the information support team. The firm specialized in human resource management and pay structures, and Anne stayed for nine years, rising to become the first female consultant.

'At that stage, I had to make a decision about what I wanted to do,' she says. She was offered a job as personnel director for a £45 million slimming business, with 4,000 consultants and staff spread across Europe. 'I took a flyer,' she says. 'I've always acted on impulse.' Within six weeks Anne was acting general manager for the German operation – she had attended German university during her years of travel – and, although it was meant to be a very temporary assignment, she stayed for nine months. 'I saw a side of life that I'd never known existed,' Anne says. Coming back after recruiting and training a new general manager, she watched as the European business bought itself out from the US parent, and sorted out the European human-resources issues for them.

In total Anne was with the company for over five years: 'In the last nine months, I thought a lot about what I ought to be doing. I had no ambition to be a board director, but I'd never considered working for myself as an option.' A colleague, Mark, suggested that they start a business together, providing tailor-made personnel and administration services for small companies that didn't need to retain the expertise in-house. They took their business plans to the bank: 'Basically,' Anne says, 'they asked, "how much do you want?"' With the facilities in place and secured by their properties, Anne resigned from her employers. 'It was a seat-of-the-pants decision,' she remembers, 'but I knew

I'd either sink or swim.' Interestingly, Anne's husband had serious reservations about her new business partner, but remained supportive.

'We were both meant to be selling,' Anne recalls, 'with Mark doing the finances and me doing product development. We won a couple of contracts very early on; we knew all the slimming companies, which were just right for our services. But Mark was clearly becoming uncomfortable with the sales work, and a lot of diplomacy was needed to deal with this problem.' Another issue was money: 'Mark was drawing far too much, and we were starting to build up an overdraft. I was putting my money to one side, but by the third quarter of our first year the cashflow situation was quite bad.' Anne came back from holiday to be confronted by Mark: 'He said that he'd been to the accountant who had told him that we'd go bankrupt if things continued as they were. I remember wondering why Mark needed to be told this by an accountant – after all, he was meant to be looking after the finances!' They agreed to keep going a little longer, even though Mark maintained that he couldn't reduce his drawings or expenses.

'I began to take more control,' Anne says. 'I hired a hotel room, and wrote to 20 managing directors of cleaning-services companies, inviting them to a conference on human resources issues. Ten of them came and, at nine o'clock on the morning after the conference, one of them rang me to invite me down to talk about management development for his company. This was business I'd always turned away in the past, but it led to a £30,000 assignment. So I dumped everything else I was doing, and slipped back into consultant mode. By this time I was really scrabbling for cash wherever I could find it. Mark wanted to break up the partnership, but he also wanted me to pay him £20,000 to go. I checked with my husband and my solicitor, prepared myself for the fight, and ended up with Mark having to pay me £15,000, plus extra expenses, and sell me his share of the business for a nominal value.' It took Anne a full year to recover financially from this partnership: 'Fortunately I was fully employed and earning money when the separation was taking place,' she says, 'so I managed to pay off the overdraft in the second year on my own.'

Now operating as a sole trader, Anne embarked upon a major sales and marketing effort. 'All my business came from cold-calling,' she recalls, 'and I did really well. By identifying market sectors I could determine what I would sell and how I would sell it. I learnt a lot about phone sales; I knew that it was a waste of time sending out letters, as they just gave people a reason to say no. You have to capture the imagination of the managing director, and hook their interest. Simply by engaging them in conversation you make a huge step towards a potential sale. I got my phone technique really well-honed, always keeping the ball in my court. And I knew that once I got in the MD's office I had a sale.'

Now in her sixth year on her own, Anne has won business from government agencies such as the TECs, even advising one TEC on the development of their own directors. All her business nowadays comes from referrals, although she expects to do more sales work, which she says she enjoys greatly. 'What I offer is good, solid human resources consultancy,' Anne says. 'I have to wonder what my competitors are up to. I always ask the question: "Why did you choose me?", and the response is normally because people think they can work with me, and that I understand their needs. That's pretty straightforward, isn't it?'

Most of Anne's time is now taken up with client-related projects, rather than administration or business development. But she is very keen to work to a schedule that suits her: 'I'm not working for myself to copy corporate workaholic practices,' she says. 'On the whole, I won't work evenings or at weekends. I'm mistress of my own destiny, and what I earn is as a direct result of my own efforts. I dictate my own quality standards and live by those.' Managing her own cash has led to a much more stable financial situation: 'Because I'm working very closely with my clients, and seeing them regularly, they tend to pay their bills promptly.'

For the future, Anne is unequivocal in her outlook. 'There's no way I'm going to be an employee again. I'm insubordinate and difficult to manage. And I'm on a professional high; I have a variety of interesting and challenging projects, and I wouldn't give that up for the world. Provided I can, I'll keep on doing what I'm doing.' As for her advice to aspiring micro-entrepreneurs, she has two cautions: 'Don't sub-contract the management of your cashflow to anyone else, and don't go into partnership with anybody else,' she advises.

Jonathan the Management Consultant

Jonathan started early – he came straight out of university to set up his own photographic products business, selling out after 30 months of successful trading. The experience taught him much about how to sell, and how to manage a business with tight margins and fierce competition. But he had become fascinated by computers and, although he was by no means computer-literate, he joined a high-flying information-services business as a management accountant. 'But I was always more interested in the commercial side of the business,' Jonathan says, and he spent time on the banking and risk-management side of the operation.

This experience led him to join a well-regarded specialist provider of services to the financial industry, a mistake he still shudders at the thought of. 'I was only there for three or four months,' Jonathan recalls, 'but it felt much longer than that. I ended up not knowing what normal was any more.' The curious management practices and motivations he came across made him deeply suspicious of employers in general and, when he was trying to get another job after realizing what a mistake he'd made, he found himself questioning everyone's motives at interviews. 'I had to go on my own, because trust was an element that was lacking,' he says now. 'Setting up my own business was definitely driven more by the push than the pull factor.'

Jonathan undertook a classic SWOT analysis of himself (see Chapter Four) – he had a good grasp of financial markets, and understood risk and its management very well. 'I was selling my consulting services at a senior level,' he recalls, 'conducting international assignments, looking at cross-border regulations and risk-management techniques. But, in all my work, I was always pushing my clients to answer the question: "What are you actually going to do?" I was prepared to help with implementation of my recommendations, but most buyers view consultancy as a justification of their own position, not as a catalyst for action.' Jonathan still wonders whether his advice was too cheap, placing a low value on it in the minds of his clients.

'I took office space too early, when rents were sky-high,' he recalls. 'That was a big mistake. And I also had an assistant to help with office administration.' But Jonathan was able to manu-facture agreements with other consultants overseas, allowing him to take a global view of the business, which he says worked very well. 'I should have developed that network more,' he believes now. When the recession started to bite in the UK things got a lot tougher. Jonathan was finding it difficult to strike the right balance between work and business development, and cashflow became more of a problem. 'I had no product that was earning money whilst I slept,' he says. 'There was a continuing sense of nervousness, but also a sense of pride.'

Then he had the Big Idea. 'I invested a lot of time and money in this, which was my biggest mistake,' he remembers. 'Venture capitalists evaluated it, but nobody in the UK was prepared to fund it. My bank was not supportive; their attitude was: "It's a nice plan but we can't help." There was no support when it really mattered. In retrospect I should have gone to the US to get funding, and I regret not doing it. Even now, people who turned me down still tell me that they were wrong, and they should have supported my idea. But the opportunity has passed.'

Disheartened by his failure to get the Big Idea off the ground, Jonathan went back half-heartedly to consulting. He got involved in a long-term project for a client who eventually offered him a job. 'I thought long and hard about it, then accepted it,' he says. 'The transition back to being an employee is extremely difficult. Managing upwards is hard work, unless your colleagues and managers are prepared to deal with you as an equal.' He is pragmatic about the move back: 'I don't view this as a career,' he believes. 'I don't worry about being fired, as I have a different perspective on life. I keep very strict hours: I'll never work at the weekend. And I'm keeping my own independence – I still contribute to a private pension plan, for instance, and have stayed divorced from office politics and the social side so that I can disengage more easily if I want to.' And Jonathan believes that this will happen: 'At some stage I'll go out on my own again,' he says, 'although I'd do things very differently next time. As soon as I can identify the level at which I can operate profitably, I'll do it.'

Jonathan feels that one of the main problems faced by sole traders is sheer loneliness. 'You need support,' he says, 'not just at home, although my wife was incredibly supportive throughout my entire life as an independent. But you want someone else to look at what you're doing and tell you that it makes sense and that they can understand what you're trying to achieve. It can be very lonely if you don't have other people to bounce ideas off.'

When and if he moves out on his own again, Jonathan is ready for the challenge. 'I now have a very good sense of my own strengths and weaknesses,' he feels. 'And the skills I've acquired could be used in any industry. The basic principles apply.'

Paul the Franchisee

Paul wanted to escape from the rat race and run a bar in Portugal. 'I'd always wanted to run my own business,' he says. 'I hate answering to other people.' But domestic complications forced him to abandon the idea of the bar only weeks before he was due to leave, and he had to take another job.

In 1989, however, he spotted an opportunity that looked perfect: he had started keeping tropical fish, and he discovered a franchise operation that would allow him to turn his hobby into a business. The franchise company took space in garden centres, where the franchisee could sell all types of fish and related equipment. Paul reckoned that he would need about £35,000 to start his own franchise but, with limited capital of his own, he needed to raise the finance elsewhere. 'I couldn't believe how easy it was with my bank,' he recalls. 'The franchise company prepared all the necessary cashflow projections and forecasts for the bank.'

Paul went to a specialist franchise adviser who told him not to proceed unless changes were made to the contract. The franchise company duly agreed to make the changes. With 1,000 square feet of retailing space, Paul was soon in business, but was rapidly discovering that the supposed benefits of being part of a franchise operation were not materializing. 'Obviously one of the main attractions of being a franchisee is that the combined operation has significant purchasing power,' he says. 'With 14 franchises in the network, this should have translated into lower costs. But in fact the designated supplier to the franchise company actually charged higher prices than other suppliers I knew.'

There were other drawbacks: 'I expected to get good advice from the franchise managing director who came to see my operation,' Paul remembers, 'but I got none. And my accountant was no use; he simply wasn't committed to my business.' Nonetheless, Paul says, 'I was still very happy in the first year on my own.' And in the second year, turnover was up by 40 per cent – but then the recession took hold.

'I had to refinance the debt with the bank,' Paul says. 'The bank was certainly getting its full benefit out of me – I always felt that it was only interested in keeping me in business so that I would continue to pay its charges.' The refinancing was expensive to put in place, and effectively lengthened the term of the loan. Support from outside was minimal: 'My family had very little understanding of what is was like for me to go through all this,' he recalls. Fortunately, Paul's wife was also in business for herself: 'Her support was unswerving,' he says.

'A part of me died during this period,' Paul says. 'I lost my sense of humour, became grumpy, and I hated going to work. I had to lay off staff, which I hated.' Ironically, the franchise company gave him the opportunity to buy another franchise: they had identified a site and had built a shop, but Paul's bank wouldn't lend him any more money and the company ended up having to run the shop. 'It went bust,' Paul remembers with some satisfaction. 'They found out what life was like for the franchisees.'

With the business now stabilized, Paul is hopeful that his past troubles are behind him. 'All I want from the business is that it breaks even, and gives me a reasonable living,' he feels. 'Once the loan is paid off things will get much better.' Paul now produces monthly information on all the sales and financial aspects of the business, which he dutifully sends to his bank. 'But I think that if the bank is making money out of you, and you're still in business, they probably don't even look at the figures,' he feels. 'The attitude of the bank has been absolutely horrendous.'

Having learnt the hard way, Paul has some very important advice for those considering taking up a franchise. 'You have to carry out every single check you can on all aspects of the business, and that includes talking to more than one other person who's done it. You should also shop around at the banks. Attitudes differ enormously.' And he believes you must be prepared for the worst: 'You must be ready to lose everything,' he advises. 'You'll need to work much harder than you ever have, and be prepared to be much poorer. So you've got to learn how to plan your cash requirements. Profit and loss isn't important – it's cash flow that matters.'

Paul was lucky, because he was able to turn a hobby into a profession, but his advice on this is stark: 'You shouldn't believe that you can turn your hobby into a business that can't fail, just because you're so committed to it. You've got to make it work.' Refreshingly, Paul is still optimistic about life as a micro-entrepreneur: 'I'd do it all again,' he maintains, 'but next time I wouldn't get into the same situation with the knowledge I now have.'

Angela the Headhunter

In spite of their reputation, headhunters (or executive-search consultants, to give them their preferred title) can fulfil a worth-while role. The best ones save companies an awful lot of time and grief, identifying potential employees who might otherwise remain undiscovered, and conducting a lot of the administrative work involved in hiring new staff.

Angela is definitely one of the best ones. With a background in marketing services, and qualifications in marketing and adver-tising, she was approached by a major US/UK search firm to set up a specialist division focusing on the advertising and public-relations industries. When she protested that she knew nothing about executive search, they responded that she didn't need to know anything – she could sell, and they would teach her the rest.

Her training ground was the City, where she built up a good client base and won major assignments. 'I always started with the managing director or chief executive,' Angela says. 'It takes the same amount of effort regardless of what level you're operating at. And I brought an international focus to the business, which was unusual for a search firm.'

After 18 months dealing with financial search, Angela was

ready to set up the specialist division she'd been hired for, but it was a City assignment that finally suggested to her that she ought to strike out on her own. 'I placed a senior manager in a financial-services company, earning the firm £80,000 in fees,' she recalls. 'My reward for this was a bonus of £500. I remember thinking, 'I don't believe this. Why do all this work for someone else for so little return?"

One evening in 1989 Angela went into the offices armed with a suitcase and took all her files, determined to work for herself. In keeping with her international bias, she decided to establish a partnership with a life-long friend who was based in Hamburg. 'She had a different background to mine, but it was obvious that with all the talk then going on in the advertising industry about cross-border associations and alliances, a continental partnership would make sense.' Angela also felt that she would broaden her remit to include mergers and acquisitions work, putting together companies who were looking for partners or outside capital and expertise.

The advertising market was still buoyant when she set up the partnership, but she experienced a major culture shock. 'I was continually asking myself: "Are these serious people?" They were so different from what I was used to in the City.' But Angela enjoyed considerable early success, pursuing her objective of starting at the top. 'I've never had a problem with opening doors,' she maintains, 'getting in to see the chairman or the MD. And I'm much more relaxed than the average headhunter, getting to know my clients really well. If you're too pushy, you just turn people off.'

In 1992 Angela made what she considers to be her biggest mistake. 'I wanted to be based in the south of France for part of the year, and I felt that I could establish my business down there. My partner had a background in film, and so the location seemed perfect. I rented an apartment in Antibes for nine weeks, and set out to research the market. I soon realized that there was very little opportunity for me. Worse still, I'd thought that I could continue to run my London operation with just a phone and a fax, but that was wrong. I was effectively out of the market, and my business suffered as a result. The timing was very bad, coming just before a recession in advertising.' Nowadays Angela tries never to leave her business for more than one week at a time.

Angela has re-established herself back in the UK, working from a home base but with a facility in the West End for when she needs to conduct interviews and meetings. 'I use hotels a tremendous amount,' she says. 'In my business, people prefer to be in a neutral location where you can wine and dine them, and I like to operate like that.' She is hoping to branch out, and is looking again at the financial-services sector. 'I would like to expand the business and take on a few key people,' she says. 'Although I enjoy the peace and seclusion I get when I come back to my home office, I do miss the environment of an office with a few people around me.'

She has established a broad network of freelance researchers to work on assignments as required: 'I'm very careful about who I will do business with,' Angela says. 'I set up associations rather than a more involved structure.' Her partnership has worked well for a simple reason: 'There's a lot of distance between us, and this physical separation is a good thing,' she says frankly. 'I don't think it would work if we were in the same office. My partner and I have a great friendship, but working in close proximity would ruin that.'

'The key to success,' Angela believes, 'is a first-class financial adviser. I use an accountant who has a complete grasp of my business, and I value his advice. I don't make a move without consulting him.' Most of her time is spent on networking, research, phoning, interviewing, and seeing new clients. 'New business development and marketing are the top priorities,' she says.

Angela knows how it feels to go it alone: 'There's always an element of risk in setting up your own business,' she admits, 'but I actually didn't have too much fear of failure. I'd effectively been working on my own when I was with my previous employer, as the division I was running was brand new. But it feels like second nature to be my own boss; I have total freedom to fit my work in around the other things that are important to me, and there's tremendous job satisfaction in knowing that everything I do is for me. The quality of my life is very important, and I'm much more comfortable being on my own. I wouldn't go back to being an employee out of choice.'

Peter the Interior Designer

This is a cautionary tale. Peter's experiences should teach you exactly how bad things can get, even when you are highly successful and extremely talented, both of which attributes Peter has in abundance.

Peter had an idea, a Big Idea, that seemed certain to make him millions and establish him as a household name. The latter he achieved, the former he most certainly did not. On a holiday in Europe he discovered a lighting technique that he believed had great potential for the UK market. Peter had been struggling to come up with a new angle for his fledgling interior-design business, something that would differentiate him from the rest of an already over-crowded market. Peter had already worked for several prestigious companies and was well qualified to offer a superior and professional service, but he needed an angle. The idea he got in Europe gave him just that. He stayed on after his holiday had finished and undertook some research on manufacturers and suppliers, as well as learning more about the product itself.

Like many successful entrepreneurs, Peter was a failure at school. 'I left school feeling I wasn't stupid, but I've always felt the need to prove to myself that I could succeed,' he says. He decided to strike out on his own when he became too frustrated with the politics of a big organization. In the mid-80s, having done the necessary deals with willing European suppliers, he opened a shop in central London which specialized in lighting products. 'I'd been taught to open up in the best area possible, but in a side street,' he says. 'Rents are much lower but you still get the right customers coming in.' The shop was meant to act as a showcase for Peter's design business, although this didn't work out quite as he'd planned.

'The whole thing went crazy,' Peter recalls, 'but only from a marketing point of view, not financially. The shop was so busy that I didn't have enough time to pursue the interior-design side of my business.' With margins very low, problems with his suppliers, and the nature of the product requiring high stock levels which were expensive to maintain, Peter realized that he needed to set up a wholesale operation that could design and manufacture his product locally. He had already had a struggle raising finance for the shop: 'I went to the banks, but my main problem was that I was proposing something new. The general reaction was that they would only back me if I could prove that someone else had already made a success of it.' One potential institutional investor insisted that he have a consultative document written that demonstrated the potential of his idea, and one of his former employers duly delivered this. But the institution took so long to make a decision that he eventually found financing elsewhere, with a private investor putting up just under half of the required equity.

When he reached the stage where he wanted to expand the operation, he got in touch with a large accounting firm that wanted to develop its links with small businesses. 'I wanted to find an investor who would give me more than money,' Peter recalls. 'I wanted to link up with someone who could offer me warehousing, and other important and expensive facilities, and who would benefit from the cachet of being linked to a strong name.' But, in spite of his best efforts, this came to nothing, and his original investor eventually introduced him to a friend. 'I was looking for about £500,000 and, to my utter astonishment, this man liked the proposal.' But his company, although able to provide the investment required, did not have any of the other facilities Peter felt a small developing business like his needed to expand successfully in a large and highly competitive market. 'I was basically forced to accept his offer, as I was very worried about how close my competitors were to catching up with me. In spite of everything that followed, I can't regret taking the investment, as I really had no alternative.'

At first things went very well. 'Although it will seem strange to some people, I had started the company on the understanding that I wouldn't mind someone else owning it as long as I could continue to develop the business,' Peter maintains. The new investor put in a finance director, and the company was set up as Peter had planned. There was a sales force, and a mail-order service, and a catalogue was produced. 'We got tremendous publicity, and our marketing was excellent,' he says. 'After six months I was very happy with what we'd achieved.' A larger shop was opened, and the business was meeting its original targets. But the new investor started to change the direction and financial plans of the company. 'Suddenly there was no money,' Peter remembers. 'We'd agreed on a phased investment plan, and I had always maintained that it would take five years to get the business to where we all wanted it. But the feedback was that the investor was losing faith in the business and had, without my knowledge, planned for a quicker return on his investment. Over a period of six to eight months, things went from bad to worse, making me feel that I'd been badly let down.'

Peter was forced into a position where many of his staff were made redundant as the money dried up, and the investor eventually cornered him and announced that he was selling the company to a major competitor, a business for which Peter had little respect. 'But I had no bad feelings about being taken over, as I felt that anything was better than what I'd been going through,' he says. 'Although technically competitors, our combined forces

gave us a major share of the market, with a much stronger chance
of success. I gave them my full support and looked forward to an
exciting future.'

However, this was not to be. 'My new partner had no
concept of business development or marketing,' he recalls. 'He
was simply a trader, taking advantage of his suppliers, using
cheap labour and running up long credit. The staff were completely demoralized.' In Peter's view, the company was not taking
advantage of a rapidly expanding market, and all his development
plans were in turmoil.

Amazingly, Peter tried to carry on with his work. He was
commissioned to write a book on the lighting technique and
began work on it. He suspects that jealousy over this book was
the main motivation behind his partner's next move. 'On the day
the book was published, he came to see me in the shop and
announced, out of the blue and with no prior warning, that I was
being made redundant,' he says. 'He demanded the keys to the
shop and I was sent home with no plausible explanation.' Peter
felt the loss deeply; as he later discovered, it was illegal to make
him redundant without following the correct consultative pro-
cedures. In Peter's case it also made no sense, as the company
traded under his name. He was unable to do any promotional
work for the book because of his contractual restrictions, causing
the publisher to lose a lot of money.

Being very practical, Peter tried to reach an amicable agreement with the company – 'a commercial divorce settlement', as
he describes it – but the company was not prepared to negotiate
on any reasonable terms. Taking expensive legal advice – which
he now considers to have been an investment in his future –
Peter filed for unfair dismissal, but he lost the preliminary hearing
on a legal technicality, and the case never came to court. The
situation was complicated by the fact that, from the start, the
company had been using his name for promotional and marketing
purposes. Peter was fully protected by a licence agreement over
the use of his name and, now he was no longer part of the

business, discussions over the company's future use of his name and wrangling over other issues that had not been thought through by his ex-partner at the time of his dismissal continued for many months.

Peter has now re-established himself, running his own business from home and involved once again with his original product, albeit in a very low-key way. He now manages to discuss the disasters and misfortunes that befell him with much humour, and has hit upon another idea that may well open up as many possibilities as the previous one. 'This time,' he avers, 'there will be no investors, and any developments will be handled by license or franchise arrangements.' Of the support he received in the past, Peter is particularly frank about the relationship with his wife. 'If I'd started the business after we were married, it would have put a great strain on the marriage,' he believes. 'But my wife knew and supported my committment to the business when we originally met, and she was unbelievably supportive through all the bad times.'

Peter's ability to continue his work independently, with full use of his name, is largely due to the high-calibre legal advice he took when starting out. Even though he owned what was a tiny company, he made sure that he had all the necessary employment and licence agreements in place. His father also gave him much sound advice. 'He told me once that the most expensive advice you can take is cheap advice,' he says, 'and that's absolutely true.'

Chandra the Marketing Adviser

Indian by birth, Chandra and her family came to Britain when she was 4. 'I wasn't academic,' she claims, 'and I flunked all my exams. But I always had a great determination to do things well, to do the best I could, from a very early age.' As a teenager Chandra got a job in a deli in south London, which turned out to be the basis of a career. 'The owner had a passion for hi-fi,' she remembers, 'and he sold equipment amongst the groceries.' At 19, Chandra went to art college, thinking that this was the line she wanted to pursue, but she returned to the business when she left college and became company secretary. 'This was how I gained my practical experience,' she says. 'You need to have worked on the shopfloor to see how things really happen in business; it's an important factor for success.'

Having opened seven branches, the proprietor eventually decided to sell up to a large hi-fi specialist chain. Chandra would liked to have been in a position to buy the business herself, but couldn't, and the deal was made contingent upon the new owner keeping her in employment. 'It was a chance to show them what I could do,' she says, 'and I stayed with them for 15 years. I became the first female retail controller, running 12 hi-fi shops.' But domestic considerations stalled her progress: she decided to get married, and she left the job to settle down as a housewife and start planning for a family.

'After two days of not working I was very bored, so I answered an advertisement for sales staff,' Chandra says. 'I just wanted something to do.' The job she took turned out to be with a large London publisher who, having realized what she could do, appointed her as special-projects manager for its specialist hi-fi magazines. She worked her way up to become a board director, in charge of marketing, after 9 years – 'I'd aimed to do it in 10!' But this meteoric rise came to an abrupt halt when she separated from her husband. 'It marked a change of direction in my life,' she recalls, 'and I needed something I could throw myself into.' The time had come for Chandra to establish her own business, and she left the publisher amicably with a one-year consultancy project from them to get her going.

'The biggest shock was the lack of discipline,' she remembers. 'I started working off the kitchen table, but soon realized that I needed a separate office which would give me that sense of going to work, and converted the garage. It's paid for itself 10 times over.' Early on she was contacted by a large food manufacturer who wanted to undertake some phone research; they hoped she might know someone who could help them. On instinct, she told them that she could do it, pitched for the business against stiff competition, and won it. Chandra hired in freelance tele-sales staff to handle the contract, and established another office in Slough, where her sister runs an employment agency.

'What I learnt from winning the contract is that marketing is marketing, regardless of the sector you're in. Ninety per cent is common sense.' When the consultancy contract with her ex-employer expired, Chandra was approached by a much bigger publisher, which had also recognised her talents. 'They wanted to develop their home entertainment business, which was an area I'd always wanted to look at before, and they gave me a contract as launch director for a new magazine.' This still allowed her to develop other business, but formed a secured financial base for her operation. 'But I've never been motivated by money,' she says. 'There has to be something beyond that – job satisfaction and achieving the most I possibly can.'

The business is now well established, but Chandra continues to keep a tight rein on expenses and income. 'Every small business must use an accountant,' she believes. 'You must pay your taxes and your VAT on time, and don't spend money you haven't got. The biggest stress for a small business comes from the money you owe, and you want to maintain good relationships with your suppliers. On the income side, I send out invoices once a month and I'm on the phone to them if they haven't paid within 14 days. I don't intend to wait for my money.'

Her success, Chandra believes, has come partly from feelings of inadequacy as a child, surrounded as she was by successful and more academic sisters. It has also come as a result of her willingness to listen to customers: 'I can operate at any level,' she says, 'and I'm very enthusiastic. I don't form quick impressions of people. You have to understand your client's needs and motivations, and put yourself in their shoes. You should never be led simply by research and statistics.' Her ambition, she says, is to make a difference: 'Chandra was here,' is how she'd like to be remembered. 'When I was working for other people, I'd always aim to double any targets set for me, because my personal goals were so high,' she recalls. 'If you're doing something you enjoy, and you make it fun, you'll undoubtedly be a success.'

'There's no more frightening prospect than starting your own business,' Chandra says. 'But you must know for yourself when you're ready to do it. People who fail are not prepared to put in the hard work to make it succeed. It's a lot more difficult than people think, and too many rush into self-employment as a result of circumstances, rather than as a conscious decision.' As an Indian woman who has been highly successful in a tough business, she has an important piece of advice: 'A lot of women in business feel that they have to be aggressive, and compete with men, just to get on. But you should first be a woman, and then show what you can do through effective results and professionalism.'

For the future, Chandra is hoping to retire within five years to spend more time with her son. 'The work I do must be of high quality, rather than quantity,' she says. 'I want the financial security to be able to give up work and sell the business, and maybe write a book about my experiences.' She is glowing about the support she has received from her friends and family. 'They've all been wonderful,' she says. She also points out that her husband gave her the necessary freedom and respect to pursue her career. 'He realized I'd be bored as a housewife, and he always treated my career as something important.'

Her advice to others is straightforward: 'It's important to remember that this is a people's world,' she says. 'You must bring the human element into sales, marketing, and everything you do – business is all about people, and you should never forget that. The same principle applies if you have employees: take care of them and they will take care of the business.'

Dee the Public Relations Consultant

'I started by accident,' Dee says, referring to the way in which she became a sole trader. 'I'd just moved house and, having lost my job, I was hoping to have the summer off.' Dee had been a marketing manager for a major US cosmetics company, and had been well trained in the art and science of American marketing techniques. She left them to become an account director for an advertising agency, a move she now regrets. 'It was the right time to move, but the wrong place to go to,' she believes. 'I was used to discipline and hard work, and the agency approach was too relaxed for me.' Returning from maternity leave, Dee stuck it out until they fired her: 'They said that the client wanted a man to handle the account, but I knew that wasn't the real reason.' Without a job, Dee's first thought was: 'What am I going to do now?'

Sitting at home, Dee was called by an old friend who had got himself into a tight situation. 'He'd committed to the launch of a new product, and had six weeks to get everything sorted out before a huge distributors' conference,' she recalls. 'He asked for my help.' That six-week assignment turned into a two-year consultancy as a public relations adviser, and Dee's business was up and running.

'I picked up bits of business here and there,' Dee remembers, 'largely through referrals. The majority of my business has always come from recommendations. Whenever I've had to put propos-als together, I've failed to win the business.' Dee's experience with proposals is instructive, suggesting that those companies that request them are merely going through the motions. 'It took me about five years to learn about proposals, and now I don't do them. With all the business I win, we have clicked personally. Referrals are immediately much more personal,' she says wisely.

Dee's transition to being her own boss has not been easy, in spite of her blue-chip client list. 'Working from home presents problems,' she says. 'You must have strong clients who believe in you and the quality of your work, regardless of where you're based. But successful public relations is a double-edged sword: it makes the companies for whom you work believe their own publicity, and feel they need a "big name" agency to handle their business. That's one of the main reasons for losing clients – but in the end, you just have to live with it.' Dee's clients tend to stay with her for a long time, and she keeps up good relations with those for whom she has worked in the past. 'One day they may come back to you, or they may refer you to other prospects,' she says.

She has been tempted to take an office and set up a small staff but has resisted it. 'If I had an office and staff I'd pick up much bigger accounts, but I'm not sure that I'd make any more money. And you have to remember why you're working for yourself – for the peace of mind, the quality of life and, above all, to be closer to your family.' Dee has no problems with the discipline required to make it work: 'The work ethic is ingrained from my time as a marketing manager.' But she has more difficulty in knowing when to change over from being a business-woman to being a mother. 'That transition period, when I come downstairs from the office, just isn't long enough. You have to learn when to cut off, because working from home can become addictive.' The fact that she is on call for her clients, and that she frequently needs to be out at early morning and evening meet-ings, has caused some problems with her husband. 'He and I had to sort things out,' Dee says, 'because he needed to see that my business is as important as his. I've had to manage my personal PR, as well as other people's!'

Dee accepts that one of the reasons for her success is her flexibility, but she says this can only go so far. 'I have to be reasonably ruthless, training clients to know what the parameters are between my work and home lives. But the goalposts are moving all the time.' Financially, she feels that working from home can be a disadvantage: 'As a woman working from home some people may think they can take you for a ride,' she believes.

'And I used to feel embarrassed about writing out invoices and asking for the money. I left my last job with a slightly bruised ego, and it took some time to learn how good I really am. Experience makes you much tougher. Getting money out of customers is a nightmare, and it now takes up an increasing amount of my time. I try and keep it friendly, but I have had to resort to sterner measures.'

One of Dee's strengths is that, in both her working and domestic life, she has learnt what she is good at. 'You have to keep your own objectives in mind all the time,' she advises. 'You must analyse what you're good at, and what you should ask someone else to do. I don't think I'd make a very good lady of leisure, for instance! It's all about horses for courses.' For the future, Dee wants to continue doing what she does now. 'Once you've learnt from your mistakes, and established your own value, you don't want to go back and be beholden to anyone else,' she maintains. 'I've made a conscious decision not to get pigeon-holed, so I will take on accounts for pots and pans as well as high fashion. But I have tended to concentrate on consumables for men and women; you must know your own limitations.'

Her biggest mistake, Dee believes, has come in the management of her assistants. 'I have always had an assistant, but I've held on to the same ones for too long,' she thinks. 'I put a lot of time and energy into training them well and, when they leave, they think they have a right to go and pinch my clients. They take some kind of reflected glory from working with me, and that's difficult to manage.' She also points out that having someone else working in your home environment presents special problems about defining the lines between the workplace and the home.

Dee's advice to budding micro-entrepreneurs is simple. 'Give it a try,' she says, 'but start with one client. You've got to get clients on board, and it's better to start off from a position of strength.'

Postscript

AND FINALLY . . .

One of your thoughts, however subliminal, whilst reading this book is likely to be: 'Who does he think he is, telling us how to run a business?' A reasonable question, I'll accept – and I have to admit to moments of doubt when I wondered why anyone would want to read what I had to say, let alone take any of the advice I've given. But I have survived on my own for three years – not without some very sticky moments – and the greater part of what I've said in this book has been validated and confirmed by the people I interviewed for the case studies. But, in the interest of authorial integrity, you should also have my own case study to pick over.

The Kindest Cut

I was fired from my last job in September 1991. Over the 15 years that I'd been in financial services I'd become increasingly unemployable, unable to manage upwards and in almost permanent conflict with my bosses over strategy, tactics and anything else that came to mind. I'd worked for five banks over those 15 years – one of them had even re-employed me after an absence of 4 years – and had lived in the Middle East, Africa, Germany and the US. My wife was always very understanding when I told her that my latest boss was a complete imbecile who fulfilled the law that states that every manager rises to their own level of incompetence.

Finally my last employer did what all the others should have done, and told me to go. It was the best thing that could have happened to me: having only been with them for 15 months, and working in a very tightly-knit sector of the banking market, my employment prospects were practically non-existent. I also knew that I was unlikely to be able to stomach any more of the corporate stupidity that I'd witnessed over those 15 years. The bank very kindly gave me a reasonable sweetener to make me go, even though they were under no obligation to do so, and I sat down with my wife one evening and worked out what I was going to do. Up until the moment I was given my P45 and shown the door, I had never once felt any desire to work for myself: I was convinced that I was too lazy to do it, that I needed the corporate safety net, and that I had absolutely nothing to offer as an independent businessman. My great leap was therefore forced on me, and nothing concentrates the mind quite as wonderfully as a solid push from your employer.

What's the Big Idea?

One of my major frustrations had always been the lack of professional sales and relationship management functions within all types of financial institution, and I was convinced that I could do something in that area. Consulting came most immediately to mind, but I'd been a consultant for a major American bank and had hated the experience: you spend weeks analysing everything to death, present your observations and recommendations, and then the report is neatly filed away by the client and never looked at again. Consultancy is hard work, too.

So I resolved to offer a training and education service, delivering customized packages to teach people at all levels about how to win and keep clients. I needed no capital to start this up, and I'd managed to retain a fairly good reputation in the industry for understanding how to deal with customers. I won some big contracts almost immediately, undertaking a customer satisfaction survey for one UK bank and training a whole division of another. But the work was pretty tedious: once you've put your training package together, and you know how to sell it and to whom, there is little real challenge in delivering it.

Customers Call the Tune

Fortunately I'd had the opportunity to write some articles for a couple of trade magazines who were always desperate for copy, and a customer read the articles and approached me with the idea of writing for them. The rationale behind this was simple: they knew I could write, they knew I understood their business and the existing and potential customers, and they couldn't fulfil all their internal and external writing commitments. Although their suggestion fell completely outside the scope of my original plan, I knew immediately that this was a better opportunity and that I would enjoy it more.

To improve matters this customer agreed to put me on a retainer. We agreed on the number of projects that would be covered by the retainer, and what work would fall outside it, and we were off. Because I did a good job for them, they referred me to another division within the bank and I started working for them, this time in areas where I didn't necessarily have the product knowledge. That was, and is, great fun: I've written marketing brochures on arcane topics such as leasing and average rate options, not only learning a lot but getting paid for it as well.

I'd started my business with an electronic typewriter and a long list of contacts I'd made during my career in the City. I sent letters to everyone I knew, telling them what I was doing and why they should consider using me. When I changed direction these people merely accepted it as a natural evolution of my business. To this day I still don't have any proper stationery or calling cards, and it hasn't been a particular drawback as far as I'm aware.

A Major Mistake – or Three

Most of the case studies demonstrate that there has been one major mistake made by the person concerned, and that they've learnt their lesson well. But I have to say that I made several mistakes, all of them major. Firstly, I have never convinced my bank that they should take my business seriously. When I started on my own I simply opened a new business account with the branch that had handled my personal account for 18 years. I never went to see the manager to explain what I was doing and why it was going to be successful. As a result, I've always been treated by the bank as a personal customer who has some other accounts; in retrospect, I should have asked to have my account in a regional business-banking centre, looked after by people who are meant to understand all about the trials of the sole trader. I don't blame the bank for the way I've been treated – they were never asked to do anything different, and were never given enough information to work on.

Secondly, I decided I needed an office. It's true that the family was living in a rather small flat and my business was taking up quite a lot of space, but the office became an unnecessary liability. I chose a serviced office, paying for privileges that I never used, in a location that was beautiful but impossible to get to by public transport. As the business grew I was rarely there, and my customers couldn't have cared less about where I did my work. The only good thing to come out of it was that I was able to leave at one month's notice.

But I left the office to move into something even worse. I had been working on a major project – my very own Big Idea – that all fell through when I realized that my potential partner was not going to be able to deliver his side of the bargain. Still depressed by my failure to get this idea off the ground, I agreed to join a partnership of consultants who had formed a loose association based around the concept that they would each contribute a share of their earnings to pay for the overheads of a

City office and full secretarial support. The concept was appealing. As all the consultants were involved in different areas of financial services there would be enormous opportunities for cross-selling, and this would lead to increased business for a relatively small outlay. I would retain my independence to work on projects that suited me, but with an improved infrastructure to support me and a professional office environment to inspire me.

The move was a disaster. Not only was I pathologically incapable of operating within even this loose partnership, but I also discovered that most of the other consultants were earning absolutely nothing. No wonder they were so keen to have me on board – I came with a nice portfolio of established clients, and they skimmed off the commission on every piece of work I did. Having imprudently written to all my contacts to tell them about this fabulous new relationship I was getting into, I then had the task of writing to them again to tell them that I was back on my own.

This all happened within my first year of business, and it certainly taught me some important lessons: I had become fiercely independent, and could no longer operate effectively with even the slightest interference or intervention of other people, however well-intentioned it might be. I had no idea that the grip of independence had taken hold so quickly and so deeply, and I just assumed that I could assimilate myself back into an office environment without any complications. I also learnt that I needed to be much more careful about who I dealt with. Although it's grossly unfair to assume that these partners only wanted me because I could bring in more money to finance the non-productive element, they certainly stood to gain an awful lot more than I did. That is not the basis on which to run a partnership.

Back to Basics

I went back to working from home, which I still do, and resolved never to have my head turned by glamorous offers of enrichment again. I now have about a dozen loyal and understanding customers who regularly give me work and pay their bills promptly. Cash flow is always going to be my major problem, as it is for almost everyone else featured in the case studies. In each of the last two years I've earnt significantly more than I did in my last job, even after expenses. I have an accountant who is one of the best in the business, and who can fight off the Inland Revenue whenever necessary. I pay him a monthly retainer so that he's on call whenever I need him. I probably pay over the odds for this privilege but, when I calculate what he has saved me and the grief from which he's protected me, I know that it's worth it.

I still haven't worked out how to get large financial institutions to pay their bills on time. I've had to threaten legal action against a particularly late payer who consistently lied to me and who, I've subsequently discovered, is legendary for screwing suppliers. It was a special pleasure to turn them down when they asked me to do more work for them, even though it meant forgoing a large chunk of income. Money continues to occupy me more than anything else, and is the subject of almost all the disagreements between my wife and me. It's not the absolute lack of it but, in common with everyone else, merely the frequency with which it appears in my account. My children long ago got used to the fact that their diet would fluctuate between excellent and rotten, and they tend to feed themselves when times are good in anticipation of the known famine that will follow!

Planning Ahead

It's about 18 months since I did any serious business development work. All my business now comes from established customers or referrals, and I continue to do a little freelance journalism to keep my name in front of potential clients. The major part of my time is actually spent on delivering copy for clients, and calling them to make sure that they're happy and haven't forgotten me.

Writing this book has made me much more aware of planning for my own future. From time to time I get offers to go back into the City, which is nice for the vanity but altogether too frightening a concept to consider seriously. But I haven't ruled out the possibility of being an employee again: if there is a single lesson to be learnt from my three years as a sole trader, it is that you should judge each opportunity on its merits. Do your due diligence, examine all the options, draw up the T-square of pluses and minuses, and then go with your gut feeling. Experience, both good and bad, teaches you to follow your instincts eventually. Too much analysis can make you disappear up your own fundament. The truly successful sole trader knows all about risk and reward, and never quite loses the sense of adventure that got them started in the first place. Going it alone is the ultimate adventure!